CHRISTIANITY: A Dictionary

Michael Keene

Stanley Thornes (Publishers) Ltd

First published in 1996 by:
Stanley Thornes (Publishers) Ltd
Ellenborough House
Wellington Street
CHELTENHAM GL50 1YW
England

96 97 98 99 00 / 10 9 8 7 6 5 4 3 2 1

A catalogue record for this book is available from the British Library.

ISBN 0 7487 2382 X

Typeset by Tech-Set, Gateshead
Printed and bound in Great Britain by Redwood Books.

Introduction

Christians are men and women who follow the teachings and example of Jesus of Nazareth. Christianity is the religious faith which expresses how these people think and feel about God. The faith which they hold is truly world-wide since it is now established in every country in the world.

Dig, though, beneath the surface of Christianity a little and you will come up with a problem. Whilst Christians share a common basic belief with each other they differ in many ways. Indeed at times you might be forgiven for thinking that you are looking at more than one religion. You only need to attend services in an Anglican, a Roman Catholic, a Greek Orthodox, a Salvation Army and a Quaker place of worship on successive Sundays to wonder just how many different forms Christianity can take. At the last count there were over 22,000 different Christian groups or denominations throughout the world. Each of them has their own distinctive slant on belief and worship.

You will find many of these differences reflected in this dictionary. It is designed to help you find your way around the most important Christian Churches and to become familiar with the different terms and words that they use. It will provide you with a short introduction to the key people, places and events which lie at the heart of Christianity – whatever form it might take. There is often a close link between one entry and another. To help you understand this – and to follow up some words – some of the words are printed in heavy type. This simply means that they have an entry all to themselves elsewhere. So, for example, take the word genuflection. If you read this definition you will find yourself being referred to:

Roman Catholics
High Church
reserved sacrament
altar
church
Pope
cardinal
bishop

With no less than eight cross-references this word is a little unusual. To make full use of the definition, however, some attempt must be made to follow up these other entries.

This dictionary contains a great deal of information. By its very nature you are only likely to use it in small doses. Keep it within reach, however, when you are studying some aspect of the Christian religion – either in general lessons or for GCSE examinations – you will find it very useful indeed.

A

Abbey originally a **church** which belonged to a religious community under the leadership of an **abbot**. Many of these communities no longer exist and the abbey has become the most important church in the **diocese**.

Abbot, Abbess the head (or superior) usually of a Benedictine monastery. The **monks** elect him for life. Benedictine **nuns** are led by an abbess. A nun must have taken her **vows** for at least ten years before she can be an abbess. She must also be over forty years old.

Abortion the planned medical removal of a foetus (baby in the early stages of development) from its mother's womb. Abortion has been legal in this country since 1967; it must be carried out before the 22nd week of pregnancy. It is condemned by all the **Christian Churches**.

Abraham a **Hebrew** who lived around 1700 BCE. He was born in Ur of the Chaldees but was led by God to Haran and then on to Canaan, which is now called **Israel**. His first son, Isaac, was born when both he and his wife, Sarah, were very old. God promised Abraham that

through Isaac, he would found a great nation. **Jews** today consider him to be the father of their nation.

Absolution forgiveness for wrong-doings (**sins**). Some **Christian Churches**, especially the **Roman Catholic Church**, teach that if a person is sorry for their sins and is determined to lead a better life in the future, then the **priest** is authorised to grant them God's absolution (forgiveness).

Abstinence a form of **penance** which usually involves going without something that is important to a person. Until 1966, Roman Catholics abstained from eating meat on Fridays as a form of **penance**. In the **Orthodox Church** there are some 150 days of abstinence in the year on which fish, meat, eggs, cheese and wine are all forbidden.

Acts of the Apostles the fifth book in the **New Testament**. This book, written by the author of **Luke's Gospel**, tells the story of the growth of the early **Christian Church**. Starting with its birth on the Day of **Pentecost**, the book mainly concerns itself with the activities of **Peter**, **John**, **Paul** and the other early Christian leaders.

An adult being baptised in a Baptist church.

Adult baptism although the **Anglican, Roman Catholic** and **Orthodox Churches** mainly baptise babies, they do have services for baptising adults as well. The **Baptist Church**, however, only baptises adults. They must make a statement of their own personal **faith** in **Christ** in front of the church members. In the service that follows they are baptised by being fully immersed in the water. ▶ See also **Believers' baptism**.

Adultery any act of sexual intercourse which takes place between a married person and someone to whom they are not married. Adultery is forbidden as one of the **Ten Commandments** given to **Moses** (Exodus 20:14) and by **Jesus** (Matthew 5:27–32). Jesus suggests that thinking about committing adultery is as bad as the act itself.

Advent comes from the Latin word meaning 'arrival'. The **Church Year** begins in December, with the season of Advent (the time of 'comings') as a preparation for the festival of **Christmas**. **Christians** use the four **Sundays** of Advent to reflect on the role of **John the Baptist** in the early ministry of **Jesus**; the **Incarnation** of Jesus and the **Second Coming** of **Christ** for which all Christians wait. The Sundays of Advent are often commemorated by the lighting of special **candles**.

Agape a love-feast from the Greek word for 'love'. Probably made up by the early **Christians** to express the special love which God has for the human race and the selfless, brotherly love which Christians were expected to have for each other. Also used to describe the shared meal, popular in the early **Church**, which was held at the same time as the **Lord's Supper**. At this meal the rich provided food for the poor in the church.

Agnus Dei in Latin the words mean the 'Lamb of God'. This is a part of the Roman Catholic **Mass** which is introduced by the ringing of the Agnus bell. It is a prayer asking God for mercy and begins with the words 'O Lamb of God, that takest away the sins of the world.'

Aisle the passage down the middle of a **church** between the **pews**.

Alb a white linen garment, worn by Roman Catholic **priests** at the **Mass**. The alb has long sleeves and reaches down to the ankles.

Alleluia a word often used in Christian **worship** to express joy and praise to God. It is left out of the **Mass** during **Lent** but is used most frequently in the **Easter** services, when **Christians** are celebrating the **resurrection** of **Jesus** from the dead.

All Saints' Day also known as 'All Hallows Day' and celebrated on November 1st. On this day **Christians** give thanks for the lives of holy men and women down the

centuries, known and unknown, who have suffered for their Christian **faith** and beliefs.

All Souls' Day takes place on the day following **All Saints Day** – November 2nd. Roman Catholics devote this day to **prayer** and **alms**-giving on behalf of those who have died. These people are believed to be in **purgatory** for the time being, where their souls are being purified by fire ready for them to enter **heaven**. In **church**, **priests** wear purple **vestments** as a sign of sorrow and hold a **Requiem Mass**.

Alms gifts for the poor. Used, particularly during the Middle Ages, to describe the collection of gifts, usually money, by the **Church** to distribute to those in need.

Alpha and Omega 'alpha' is the first letter and 'omega' the last letter of the Greek alphabet. The phrase is used in the **Bible** to describe **Jesus** as the beginning and end. The two letters together were used by early **Christians** on monuments, tombstones and coins.

Altar from the Latin word meaning 'high'. The holy table where the **bread** and wine used in **Holy Communion** are blessed and offered up to God. It represents the table at which **Jesus** shared his last meal with his **disciples**. By the 5th century, stone altars were found in Christian piaces of **worship**. For a long time they were placed against the east wall in a **church** but in

This is a traditional Roman Catholic altar.

modern churches they are often free-standing and placed in the middle of people.

Alternative Service Book
the new official Prayer Book authorised for use in the **Church of England** in 1980. The *Alternative Service Book*, or *ASB* as it is commonly called, contains three forms of the **Eucharistic** service, together with shortened forms of **Morning Prayer** (Matins) and **Evening Prayer** (Evensong). It has been used alongside the **Book of Common Prayer** although it has now replaced it in many **churches**. This was not the original intention of publishing a new Prayer Book.

Amen all Christian **prayers** end with this word which means 'truly'.

It is used to express the whole-hearted agreement of those taking part in the act of **worship**.

Andrew a fisherman and the brother of **Peter**. One of the original **disciples** who, as he was fishing, was called by **Jesus** to follow him. According to tradition, he died by being crucified.

Angel based on several references in the **Bible**, the **Church** has long accepted the existence of angels – good and bad. They were originally created good by God but some rebelled before the creation of the world. They then gave their support to **Satan** as their leader. In the **Bible**, angels are the messengers of God – most notably in the events leading up to the birth of **Jesus** (Matthew 1:18–25; Luke 2:8–14).

Angel Gabriel
one of the archangels (chief angels) of Christian belief but the only one mentioned in the **New Testament**. Gabriel figures in the **Old Testament** (the Book of Daniel), looks forward to the birth of **John the Baptist** (Luke 1:18–20) and announces the conception of **Jesus** to the **Virgin Mary** (Luke 1:26–38).

Anglican Communion
the world-wide fellowship of different **Churches** which are based on the teachings of the **Church of England**. They all accept the leadership of the **Archbishop** of Canterbury. The Anglican Communion includes the **Church of England** and others, such as the Church of Australia and the Church of Canada. **Bishops** from the Anglican Communion come together once every ten years for the Lambeth Conference at Lambeth Palace, the residence of the Archbishop of Canterbury.

Anglo-Catholics
also known as 'High Church'. Their existence in the **Church of England** goes back to the **Reformation** in England which put an end to the power of the **Pope** in **Rome** over the **Church** in England. Ever since, there have been members of the Church of England who have still followed patterns of **worship** similar to those of the **Roman Catholic Church**. In recent years the strength of this group within the Church of England has declined. Many have joined the Roman Catholic Church because they have disagreed with the decision to ordain women.

Annunciation
a festival held in the **Roman Catholic Church**, on March 25th. It marks the visit of the **Angel Gabriel** to the **Virgin Mary** and the conception in her womb of **Jesus** (Luke 1:26–38). It was on this visit by the **angel** that Mary learned that she had been chosen by God to bear his son, Jesus Christ.

Anointing
smearing with blessed or consecrated **oil**. This is done by the **Roman Catholic Church** in the ceremonies of anointing at **baptism, confirmation** and **extreme unction**. The early **Church** anointed people and prayed over them for **healing**. This practice has been revived in recent times.

Anthem
a piece of choral **music** that is sung in **church** with words taken from the **Bible**.

Anti-Semitism
feelings of hatred and hostility directed specifically towards the **Jews**. This hatred has often come from the **Christian Church** because **Christians** have always held the Jews responsible for the death of **Jesus** – an attitude based largely on Matthew 27:25.

Apartheid
a word used to describe the South African government's policy between 1948 and 1994 of racial segregation and the separate development of the different races (white, black and

coloured). Widely condemned throughout the world by **Christians** and others, apartheid found strong support from the Dutch Reformed Church in South Africa itself. The policy was abandoned in 1994 when a general election brought the black leader, Nelson Mandela, to power. ▶ See also **racism**.

Apocrypha this comes from the Greek word meaning 'hidden'. It refers to a collection of books which the **Jews** do not include in their **Scriptures**. The **Roman Catholic Church**, however, follows the example of Jerome (342–420) in accepting these books as part of their Scriptures. There are seven in the **Jerusalem Bible** (1966), including 1 and 2 Maccabees, the Book of Wisdom and Ecclesiasticus.

Apostle the word itself, from the Greek 'to send', was applied to the original twelve **disciples** after the death and **resurrection** of **Jesus**. The Apostles were those who were 'sent out' into the world by God to preach the Good News (the **Gospel**) of Jesus.

Apostles Creed the oldest statement of **faith** in the **Christian Church**. It falls into three sections dealing with God the **Father**, God the Son, and God the **Holy Spirit**. Whilst not written by the **Apostles** themselves, the Creed would seem to go back to the 2nd or 3rd centuries. It is still used by some **Churches** as part of their **worship**. The Apostles Creed in full is on page 82.

Apostolic blessing the **blessing** given by the **Pope** at the end of **Mass** on very special occasions – especially **Easter**.

Apostolic succession the belief that in the early **Church**, the **Apostles** passed on the truth about **Jesus**, as well as their authority to preach God's message, to those who followed them. Such authority was then passed down from one **bishop** to another through the '**laying on of hands**'. This was called apostolic succession. In this way, the **Roman Catholic** and **Orthodox Churches** could claim that their leaders were in a direct line of succession from the original Apostles. The belief soon developed that only those people ordained had the authority to administer the **sacraments**. ▶ See also **ordination**.

Aramaic the language spoken by everyone in **Palestine** at the time of **Jesus** – and the language in which he almost certainly taught. Although the **Gospels** were written in Greek, a few Aramaic phrases are still to be found – like *Talitha Cumi* in Mark 5:41 and *Ephphatha*.

Archangel an angel of the highest rank. In the **Bible** this title is only given to **Gabriel** and Michael. These two archangels are the main opponents of **Satan** and his followers. They are given special tasks to perform by God. In particular, Gabriel was chosen to bear messages to individual human beings on more than one occasion.

Archbishop the chief **bishop** in the **Church of England** and the **Roman Catholic Church** who has authority over the other bishops under his supervision. In the Church of England, there are two archbishops – of Canterbury and of York. Between them they are responsible for the various activities of all **dioceses** in the Church of England in Great Britain. The Archbishop of Canterbury takes precedence over the Archbishop of York. There are historical reasons why the **see** of Canterbury is the most important in England.

Archdeacon an official in the Church of England, next under a **bishop**. In each **diocese** archdeacons are appointed to visit **parishes** and present candidates for **ordination**. To be an archdeacon, a **priest** must have been ordained for more than six years.

Ascension Day this is observed by some **Churches** on the sixth Thursday, i.e. the fortieth day, after **Easter Day**. In the **Roman Catholic Church**, Ascension Day is a **feast of obligation**. ▶ See also **Ascension of Christ**.

Ascension of Christ **Christians** believe that the life of **Jesus** on earth ended 40 days after he rose from the dead when he ascended, or went up, into **heaven**. Both Luke 24 and the **Acts of the Apostles** describe this. ▶ See also **Ascension Day**, **Resurrection**.

Ash Wednesday the first day of **Lent**, the 40-day period of **fasting** which leads up to **Easter**. In some **churches**, during a service the **priest** makes the mark of the **cross** with ash on the foreheads of worshippers as a symbol of their humility and the desire they have to be forgiven by God. This ash comes from the burning of the previous year's palm crosses. As he applies it, the priest says, 'Dust you are and to dust you shall return'. ▶ See also **Palm Sunday**.

Assumption of the Virgin Mary this festival, which is held in **Roman Catholic** and **Orthodox Churches** on August 15th each year, recalls the taking up of the **Virgin Mary**, body and soul, into **heaven** at the end of her life. The belief can be traced back to the 6th century. In 1950 Pope Pius XII made it a **dogma** of the **Church**. In the **Eastern Orthodox Church**, this is known as the **dormition** (falling asleep) **of the Virgin**.

Atheism not believing in the existence of God. Early **Christians** were called atheists by the Greeks and Romans because they refused to believe in their gods.

Atonement in the **Bible**, the word is used to describe the bringing together (reconciliation) of God and the human race. **Sin** came between God and human beings, but through the death of **Christ**, the relationship has been made good again.

Augustine of Canterbury

(died c.604) a **monk** appointed by Pope Gregory I to lead 40 other monks in bringing the Christian **Gospel** to England from **Rome**. They landed in Kent in 595 and were soon given the land of **Canterbury** as their base by King Ethelburt. Their work was so effective that before the end of the 7th century all the Saxon kingdoms had turned to **Christianity**. Augustine became the first **Archbishop** of Canterbury.

Authorised Version

this translation of the **Bible** was authorised by King James I and published in 1611. Fifty-four scholars, working in six groups, produced what has long been accepted as one of the masterpieces of the English language. It is still used in many **churches**, although in others it has been replaced by more modern translations, such as the **Good News Bible** or the *Revised English Bible*. Since 1984 it has been called the *Authorised King James Version*.

Ave Maria

this is a **prayer** addressed to the **Virgin Mary** and widely used in Roman Catholic **worship** – where it is often called the **Hail Mary**. It falls into two parts: **a** the first part is taken directly from Luke 1:28–42. **b** the second part is 'Holy Mary, Mother of God, pray for us sinners now and at the hour of our death.' The phrase is repeated when saying the **rosary**. See page 83 for the full prayer.

B

Banns of marriage

the custom of announcing a forthcoming **marriage** during an Anglican morning service developed in the early Middle Ages. The purpose was to prevent possible bigamy (people marrying when they already have a husband or wife). Today marriage banns are read in the home **parish** of each partner on three successive **Sundays** shortly before they marry.

Baptism

the **sacrament** in which people – children or adults – become members of the **Christian Church**. To Roman Catholics, Anglicans and Orthodox believers, baptism is a sacrament. The water used is a

symbol of cleansing and rebirth.
▶See also **adult baptism, infant baptism, initiation**.

Baptism in the Holy Spirit an expression used by Pentecostal and Charismatic Christians, referring to an overwhelming experience by which they have been filled with the **Holy Spirit**. It comes after a person has been converted to **Christ**. It is usually accompanied by the person 'speaking in tongues'. ▶See also **Charismatic Movement, Pentecostal Movement**.

Baptist Church one of the largest world-wide **Protestant denominations**. Membership of the Baptist Church, which began in Amsterdam in 1609, is only open to adult Christian believers who have expressed their faith in **Jesus Christ** as Saviour and have been baptised. The Baptists emphasise acceptance of the **Bible** as the Word of God. ▶See also **adult baptism, believers' baptism**.

Baptistry a building or the part of a building in which a **baptism** is carried out. Although baptistries were built in very early **churches**, before **infant baptisms** were carried out in **fonts**, they are now confined to **Baptist** churches. They are normally built underneath the floorboards at the front of the church.

Barabbas according to the **Gospels** Barabbas was the criminal who was released to the crowd at the time when **Jesus** was condemned to death by **Pontius Pilate**.

Basilica originally a royal palace but later came to mean a large building with a **nave** and **aisle**. Some of these buildings were adapted by the early **Christians** for use as **churches**. The most famous basilica of all is St Peter's in **Rome**.

Beatific vision a glimpse of the glory of **heaven**. In the **Beatitudes**, **Jesus** told his followers: 'Blessed are those whose hearts are pure; they shall see God.' (Matthew 5:8). Roman Catholics believe that this promise is fulfilled when the righteous reach heaven after spending time in **purgatory**. In heaven they enjoy a continual, and everlasting (eternal), sense of God's presence.

Beatification the first step towards a person becoming a **saint** in the **Roman Catholic Church**. A deceased person is declared by the **Pope** to be one of the 'blessed departed'. After being beatified, a person is normally given the title 'Blessed'. Beatification is usually, but not always, a step towards **canonisation**.

Beatitudes promises made by **Jesus** of present and future **blessings** to people who show particular spiritual characteristics (Matthew 5:1–12). Jesus singled out nine such groups – and promised them blessings on earth or in **heaven**. The Beatitudes in full are on page 84.

Beelzebub this is the name applied to the 'Prince of devils' in the **Gospels** (Matthew 12:24). On one occasion **Christ**'s enemies accused him of 'casting out devils by Beelzebub' (Mark 3:22–26). Elsewhere Beelzebub is called **Satan** or simply the **Devil**.

Believers' baptism most of the **Christian Churches** – including the **Anglican**, **Roman Catholic** and **Orthodox Churches** – baptise infants, although they do occasionally baptise adults. The **Baptist Church** and a few other **Nonconformist Churches**, however, baptise only adults, who must make a public confession of their personal trust and **faith** in **Jesus Christ** first. Believers are normally lowered beneath the water in a **baptistry** (a pool at the front of a church) although some are baptised in a river or the sea. ▶See also **adult baptism, infant baptism**.

Bema a platform. In an Eastern Orthodox **church** it is the enclosure which contains the **altar**, raised above the level of the **nave** and shut off by the **iconostasis**.

Benedictines Benedictines are **monks** or **nuns** belonging to an order (religious group) which follows the Rule and teaching of St

Benedict (480–c.550). The order, which was formed around 530, attaches great importance to staying in the same **monastery**; holy learning; living a life of communal and private **prayer** and obeying the **abbot** or **abbess**. Dressed in their traditional black **habit** (clothes), the Benedictines have probably been the most influential of all monastic orders. Many other religious orders have followed the Rule of St Benedict with its emphasis on poverty, **chastity** and obedience.

Benediction 1 the **blessing** (a pronouncement of God's favour), usually spoken from the altar, by the **priest** or **minister** at the end of a service: 'The blessing of God Almighty, Father, Son and Holy Spirit be with you ….' **2** a short service in the **Roman Catholic Church** after which the priest makes the **sign of the cross** over the congregation with the **host**.

Benedictus the first word in Latin of the hymn of thanksgiving of Zacharias on the birth of his son, **John the Baptist** (Luke 1.68–70). The hymn is used in the **Roman Catholic Church** and praises God, saying, 'Blessed be the Lord God of Israel'.

Bernadette, Saint (1844–79) a French peasant girl who, at the age of 14, received 18 visions of the **Virgin Mary** at the Massabiele Rock, near **Lourdes**. The visions predicted that a spring would rise from the grotto floor. When a spring appeared, people believed that it had **healing** properties. A **church** was built on the rock. Bernadette was canonised (made a saint) and Lourdes became the main **pilgrimage** destination for Roman Catholics. ▶ See also **canonisation**.

Bethlehem a small town five miles south of **Jerusalem**. It was the birthplace of King David and **Jesus**. The **Church** of the Nativity stands on the supposed site.

Bible the sacred book for **Christians**. It is in two parts – the **Old Testament** and the **New**

Testament. The Old Testament contains 39 books and also forms the sacred **Scriptures** for all **Jews**. In the 27 books of the New Testament there are: **a** Four **Gospels**; **b** the **Acts of the Apostles**; **c Epistles** (letters) written by **Paul**, **Peter**, James and **John**, among others; **d** the Revelation, also written by John.

Bishop the office of bishop is traced all the way back to the original **Apostles** by some **Churches**. In those **Churches**, bishops alone have the authority to conduct **confirmations** and **ordinations**. The outward signs of a bishop are a mitre (a hat rising to two points with a cleft between them), crozier

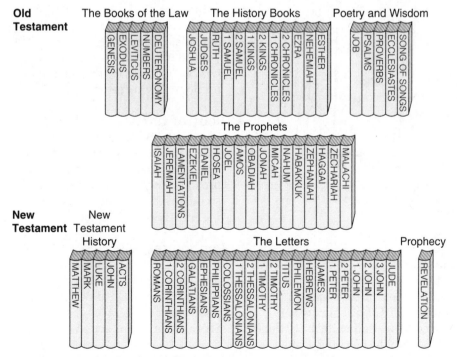

The whole Bible is made up of 66 books, covering many different kinds of literature as you can see.

(crook-shaped staff), pectoral **cross** (a cross suspended by a chain around the neck) and ring. An 'episcopal' Church is one in which bishops have responsibility for churches in a particular **diocese.** ▶ See also **apostolic succession.**

The Anglican Roman Catholic and Orthodox Churches are all episcopal churches – they have bishops.

Blasphemy any form of words or actions which show contempt for God. In the **Old Testament**, a person found guilty of blasphemy was stoned to death (Leviticus 24:16). In England in the 16th and 17th centuries, it was punished very severely.

Blessing the pronouncement of God's favour upon a **church** congregation or an individual worshipper. Many church services end with a blessing being given by the **priest**, usually from the steps of the **altar.** ▶ See also **benediction.**

Blood a symbol of life. The blood of **Jesus** is represented at the service of **Holy Communion** by the wine which all the worshippers share in drinking. Roman Catholics believe that during the **mass** the wine becomes the actual blood of Jesus, and the **bread** his body. ▶ See also **body of Christ.**

Boanerges a name meaning 'sons of thunder' (Luke 4.54; Mark 3.17). It was given to James and **John**, the **disciples** of **Jesus**, because they wanted to call down 'fire from **heaven'** to consume the Samaritans for not receiving Jesus.

Body of Christ a term which is used in the **Bible** in two different ways. **1** as an image of the **Christian Church** (Romans 12.5). **2** of the **bread** in **Holy Communion** which, some Christians believe, becomes the actual body of **Christ.**

Bonhoeffer, Dietrich (1906–45) a German Lutheran **minister** who was arrested in 1943 for taking part in a plan to assassinate Adolf Hitler. He was hanged a few weeks before the Second World War ended in 1945.

Book of Common Prayer this authorised prayer book of the

Church of England was first drawn up during the time of the **Reformation** under **Thomas Cranmer** in 1649. Three versions were used during the 16th century, with a revision in 1662 which is still used in many **churches** today. The Book of Common Prayer has been replaced in many churches by the **Alternative Service Book** since 1980.

Booth, William (1829–1912) the founder and first general of the **Salvation Army**. In 1865, he founded the Christian Mission to preach the **Gospel** and carry out social and rescue work in the East End of London. In 1878, the Salvation Army was formed and organised on military lines. Since then the Army has spread into almost 200 countries.

Bread just as bread is a basic food necessary for life, so is Christ the 'bread of life' (John 6.35), giving spiritual nourishment. The bread and wine during the **Eucharist** symbolise the **body** and **blood** of **Jesus**.

Breaking of bread one of the favourite terms used by **Nonconformists** to describe the service of **Holy Communion**. In 'breaking **bread**' (literally breaking open a loaf) together, they remember the death and **resurrection** of **Jesus** and recall that in the time of Jesus, friends often met together 'to break bread' (eat a simple meal). It expressed their close friendship with

each other. The 'Breaking of Bread' service symbolises the close friendship between **Jesus** and all true believers.

Brethren also known as the Plymouth Brethren, this **denomination** first appeared in Plymouth in 1830. They do not agree with **Church** organisation of any kind, building their **worship** around **baptism** and **breaking of bread**. In 1845, a Strict Brethren group was formed forbidding members to associate with other **Christians** or for non-members to attend their meetings.

Breviary a book which contains the daily services of the **Roman Catholic Church**. **Priests** are bound by the **vows** that they took on **ordination** to follow these services. The breviary does not contain the service of **Mass** since that is found in the **Missal**.

Burial the traditional Christian way of disposing of the bodies of the dead. Burial can be in the ground, in a cave or at sea. An area of graves together is called a cemetery. **Christians** believe that the bodies of all believers will be brought back to life at the **second coming** and so burial seems more in keeping with this belief than cremation (burning). In recent years, though, cremation has become much more widely practised.

C

Caesarea Philippi a small town at the foot of Mount Hermon where **Peter** told **Jesus** that he knew he was the **Messiah** everyone had been waiting for (Matthew 16:16).

Caiaphas the Jewish **High Priest** at the time of **Christ**. **Jesus** was tried before Caiaphas before being taken in front of **Pontius Pilate** (Matthew 26:3).

Calvary the place close to **Jerusalem** where **Jesus** was crucified. It is also known as Golgotha, the **Hebrew** word for 'skull', because of the shape of the rock.

Calvinism the teachings and beliefs of the great Swiss religious reformer, John Calvin (1509–64). He taught that God is all-powerful, men and women are totally sinful and that God chooses some people to be saved.

Candle these are used in many **Churches** – especially **Roman Catholic**, **Orthodox** and **High Church Anglican**. They are placed on the **altar** during **worship**. Votive candles are lit in front of statues in Catholic and Orthodox churches and at **shrines** before personal **prayers**

are said. In many churches a **Paschal candle** brings light into a dark church at the beginning of the first service held on **Easter Day**. As symbols, candles represent the light of God shining in a dark and sinful world.

Candlemas the festival which commemorates the presentation of **Jesus** in the **Temple** to God a few days after he was born (Luke 2:22ff.). There is a traditional blessing of **candles** on this day during the special **Eucharist** service. These candles are then used in **church** during the year to symbolise **Jesus** as the 'light of the world'.

Canon of Scripture those books which the **Church** accepts as carrying the authority of God. By the end of the 1st century CE, the books to be included in the **Old Testament** canon were agreed. Most of the books in the **New Testament** canon were agreed by 130 CE. By the end of the 4th century all the books in the **Scriptures** were agreed. The canon has remained unchanged ever since.

Canonisation the decision taken by the **Pope** that a dead member of the **Roman Catholic Church** should be listed amongst the **saints**. This means that he or she is thought to be worthy of the greatest respect and reverence. The person can then be called upon in **heaven** to pray for sinners on earth. ▶See also **beatification**.

Canterbury the place where **St Augustine**, sent to England to preach the **Gospel** by Pope Gregory I, set up his first **church**. Agustine was made the first **Archbishop of Canterbury** by the **Pope** in 598. Canterbury has remained at the centre of the church in England ever since.

Canticle a short **hymn** or **chant** taken from the **Bible**. The **Roman Catholic** and **Anglican Churches** include canticles, such as the **Te Deum**, in their services.

Capital punishment when a person is put to death for committing a particularly serious crime. Over the centuries the **Church** has generally supported capital punishment. **Paul**, for example, seems to have accepted it (Romans 13:1–5). Even today when many people do not agree with it, few Churches have come out against it – with the exception of the **Quakers**. There is no capital punishment in Britain.

Cardinal one of the **priests** holding the highest rank in the **Roman Catholic Church** below that of the **Pope**. A cardinal can only be appointed by the Pope and receives a

biretta – a rigid red square cap – as a symbol of his position (office). If a Pope dies, together the cardinals form the Sacred College with responsibility for electing his successor.

Carmelite an order of **friars** which began in the 12th century and took its name from Mount Carmel in Syria. Wearing a white mantle the Carmelites are also known as the 'White Friars'. In 16th century, the order was reformed to include **nuns**.

Carol originally a round dance but later it was the name given to a happy **hymn** with words associated with the birth of **Jesus**. Now used for any hymns which take the birth of Jesus in **Bethlehem** as their theme.

Cassock a long, close-fitting robe worn by **priests** and others while they are taking part in **church** services. The robe reaches down to the heels and is usually black. **Bishops**, though, wear purple cassocks, **cardinals** red ones and the **Pope** a white cassock.

Catechism a book of Christian belief which is designed to help those who are having instruction before they are baptised or confirmed. Traditionally, it is written as a conversation between a teacher and a pupil. However, the recent *Catechism of the Catholic Church* is a straightforward account of Roman Catholic beliefs.

Catechumen in the early **Church**, a man or woman undergoing training and preparation before being baptised. This training took place throughout **Lent** before **baptism** at the Easter Vigil. Roman Catholics reintroduced this training for adults wanting to be baptised in 1972.

Cathedral the main **church** in the **diocese** of a **bishop** which contains the bishop's cathedra (chair or throne). This is usually placed in the **chancel** – in front of the **altar** and choir stalls.

Celibacy means the acceptance of the single life as a gift from God, from the Latin word for a 'bachelor'. Both **monks** and **nuns** take a **vow** of celibacy as do Roman Catholic **priests**. In the **Orthodox Church**, priests may marry if they do so before they are ordained. **Protestants** accept marriage as the normal state for both priests and **laity**.

Chalice the cup, usually made of silver, which holds the wine during **Holy Communion**. This wine is a symbol of the **blood** of **Christ**. The **bread**, as a symbol of the **body of Christ**, is placed on a **paten**. Roman Catholics believe that the bread and wine actually become the body and blood of Christ during the Mass.
▶See also **real presence**.

Chancel the part of a **church** where the **altar** and the stalls in which the **choir** and **clergy** sit are to be found. In many older churches, a screen (the rood screen) separated the chancel from the **nave**, although most of these screens have long since been removed.

Chant a melody or a song of a slow kind with a long note on which words are recited. 'Gregorian chants' are the most well-known, named after St Gregory the Great.

Chapel 1 the name usually given to a **Nonconformist** place of worship e.g. **Methodist** chapel, **Baptist** chapel, etc. **2** inside large **churches** and **cathedrals**, side chapels are often found with their own **altars**. These are often dedicated to **saints** – especially the **Virgin Mary**.

Chaplain an ordained **priest** who does not have a **parish** to look after. Instead he or she could be responsible for the spiritual welfare of, say, a factory, a school, a prison or even a shopping precinct. Regiments in the Armed Forces also have their own chaplains who travel with them wherever they are posted.

Charismatic Movement a modern religious movement found within the Roman Catholic Church and Protestant **denominations**. Those who belong to it share a common belief in an experience of the **Holy Spirit** which often results in '**speaking in tongues**', **healings** and **prophecies**.

Chastity keeping sexually pure. This covers the sexual behaviour of people in all walks of life – including virgins, partners within marriage, and widows or widowers who have not remarried. Chastity is destroyed by **fornication** and **adultery**. **Monks** and **nuns** take a **vow** of chastity when they become members of their religious order.

Chasuble the main garment worn by **bishops** and **priests** when they are celebrating **Holy Communion**. It is a rectangular sleeveless garment with a hole in the middle for the head. It hangs down both front and back.

Choir a group of singers who have been trained to sing together in church services. Traditionally church choirs have been all male, singing very beautiful music – often in parts – specially written for the range of male voices. Now, however, the vast majority are also open to women. Sometimes a choir may sing to the congregation, whilst on other occasions it sings with them. Members of a choir usually wear a **surplus** over a **cassock**.

Chrism from the Greek 'to anoint', this is the holy **oil** used on special occasions in the **Roman Catholic** and **Orthodox Churches**. A mixture of olive oil and balsam chrism is used, especially in **baptism** services, symbolising the giving of the **Holy Spirit** to the person receiving the **sacrament**. ▶ See also **anointing, chrismation**.

Chrismation after a baby has been baptised in the **Orthodox**

Church, it is anointed by the **priest**. Oil is wiped on its forehead, eyes, lips, mouth, nostrils, breast, hands and feet. As the priest does so, he says to the baby '... the seal of the Holy Spirit', emphasising that the baby's receiving of the **Holy Spirit** is its guarantee of eternal life.

Christ the name means 'the Anointed One'. It is the Greek form of the **Hebrew** word **Messiah**. It was soon used by the followers of the risen **Jesus** as a proper name. This is why the first followers of Jesus became known as **Christians**.

Christening the ceremony in which a person, usually a baby, is received into the **Church** by **baptism** and given a name.

Christian someone who is committed to the Christian religion and the Christian **faith**. According to Acts 11:26, the term Christian was given to the early followers of **Jesus** to distinguish them from **Jews** and other religious groups of the time.

Christian Church this embraces all followers of **Jesus Christ** world-wide. It includes all **denominations** which believe in the **Trinity**, Jesus Christ and the **Holy Spirit**. There are over 5,000 such denominations.

Christianity the religion of the followers of **Jesus Christ**, based firmly on his teachings. It includes all **Churches** which accept Jesus Christ as Son of God, Lord and Saviour. Christianity has more

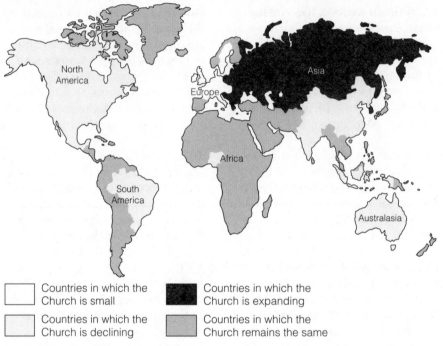

□ Countries in which the Church is small

■ Countries in which the Church is expanding

▨ Countries in which the Church is declining

▨ Countries in which the Church remains the same

Christianity has followers all over the world.

followers world-wide than any other religion.

Christmas the festival held by **Christians** to celebrate the birth of **Jesus** in **Bethlehem**. The date, December 25th, does not have any real significance. It was taken over in 336 CE from the Roman festival of 'Natalis Solis Invicti' when the birth of the 'Sun of Righteousness' was celebrated. No one knows exactly when Jesus was born.

Church this has two closely related meanings: **1** the name given to various communities or groups of Christian believers throughout the world. Although each acknowledges **Jesus Christ** as Lord, they are often organised in very different ways with different styles of **worship**. **2** the buildings in which many **Christians** carry out their worship.

Church Army an Evangelical organisation within the **Church of England** which was founded by Wilson Carlisle in 1882. It began its work among the poor in the East End of London, along similar lines to the **Salvation Army**. Like them, the Church Army wears a distinctive uniform. ▶See also **Evangelism**.

Church of England in the 16th century, King Henry VIII quarrelled with the **Pope** because the King wanted to **divorce**. Afterwards, he broke all ties with the **Church** of **Rome** and the Church of England was formed with the King instead of the Pope as its head. The **monasteries**, the real source of Rome's power in England, were closed down. Under Elizabeth I, the Church of England became the **Established** (official) **Church** in England, which it remains today.

Churchyard an enclosed area surrounding a **church**, often used as a burial ground. In the Middle Ages, churchyards were often also used for celebrations and festivals.

Church Year the calendar of annual festivals followed by the **Anglican**, **Roman Catholic** and **Orthodox Churches** who use it as the pattern for their **worship** week by week. It begins with the season of **Advent** and runs through **Christmas**, **Easter** and **Whitsun**. There are also many smaller festivals throughout the year which some of the Churches celebrate.

Circumcision the practice of cutting away the foreskin on a boy's penis. It is compulsory for Jewish males and done when the baby is eight days old. It became an important issue in the Early Church when many non-Jews (**Gentiles**) were converted to **Christianity** and did not know if they should be circumcised before they could be accepted as full members of the **Church**. The church leaders met together in **Jerusalem** (in 50 CE) and decided that it was not necessary. At the same time Gentile **Christians** were told to abstain

December

ADVENT
CHRISTMAS
EPIPHANY
LENT
September
SUNDAYS AFTER TRINITY
HOLY WEEK
March
EASTER
ASCENSION
WHITSUN
TRINITY
June

The Church Year showing the annual festivals celebrated by the Church.

from any religious practice that might offend Jewish Christians.

Citadel a small, fortified city. The word is used by the **Salvation Army** for their places of **worship**. Citadels have always offered spiritual and physical safety from the wicked world outside. As the Salvation Army established itself in some of the most deprived parts of the country, this connection was important to the early Salvationists.

Clergy the group of ordained people in any of the Christian **denominations**. Their main task is a pastoral one – they have a flock of people (congregation) to look after and care for. In the modern **Church**, as the **Second Vatican Council** emphasised, the **laity** are as important as the clergy – they simply have a different role to perform. ▶See also **ordination, Second Vatican Council**.

Collect a short, set **prayer** contained within the Anglican Prayer Book and the Roman Catholic **Missal**. Regular collects are used week by week. There are also special ones only used on particular feast days. Although many go back to medieval times, some were written by **Thomas Cranmer** especially for the **Book of Common Prayer**. In the **Eucharist** service the Collect is said before the **Epistle** is read.

Communion of Saints 1 the fellowship that exists between Christ and every Christian believer. 2 the fellowship between every **Christian**

– whether they are on earth, in **purgatory** or in **heaven**. It is in the **Apostles Creed** (see p. 00) as part of the statement of belief of Christians: 'I believe in the Communion of Saints'.

Communion table in **Nonconformist churches** this replaces the **altar** at the front of the congregation. It is from this table that the most important service – the **Breaking of Bread** – is conducted by the **minister** who faces the people.

Compline the last service of the day which is said around 8 p.m or 9 p.m in some Anglican **churches**. It is so called because it 'completes' the regular daily cycle of services.

Compostela Santiago de Compostela is the city in Spain where the bones of St James the Great are believed to be preserved. Since the 10th century it has been a popular place of **pilgrimage** for Roman Catholics.

Conclave a private room. It refers specifically to the group of **cardinals** who meet together in private to elect a new **Pope**. The number of cardinals present for the election cannot be more than 120 and one of their number will be chosen as Pope.

Confession **prayer** offered to God whilst admitting one has done wrong and expressing a deep sorrow for it. In the **Roman Catholic Church** this confession is made through a **priest**. After someone has shown that they are sorry, the priest gives them **absolution** (forgiveness). He may also ask the person to do a **penance** (a punishment) usually in the form of **prayers**. The seal of confession binds a priest not to make public anything that he has learned in the confessional.

Confirmation ritual celebrated in **Anglican** and **Roman Catholic Churches** when a person is believed to receive the **Holy Spirit**. This happens through the **laying on of hands** by a **bishop**. It marks the completion of a process which began with **baptism** as a baby. After confirmation a person is accepted into full church membership. In the Anglican Church, people can receive the **Eucharist** only after confirmation, but in the Roman Catholic Church they can take **Holy Communion** before.

Congregationalists a branch of the **Nonconformists**. Each member of the **church** is given equal rights. In 1972 the Congregationalists in England merged with the Presbyterians to form the **United Reformed Church**.

Conscientious objection when a person cannot take part in a particular activity because it would be against their conscience to do so. This is most likely to occur when someone is called upon to fight in a war and yet they have strong moral or religious objections to doing so. There were many conscientious objectors in Britain during the First World War (1914–18) and Second World War (1939–45). ▶See also **pacifism**.

Consecration the act by which things or people are set aside for holy use. For example: **bread** and wine are consecrated before they are shared with the people in **Holy Communion**; a **church** is consecrated before it is used for **worship**; a **bishop** is consecrated before he takes up his new work.

Constantine (c.274–337) the first Christian Emperor of **Rome** who established **Christianity** as the religion of the State. He is said to have been converted on the eve of a battle with his greatest rival when he saw a flaming **cross** with the words in Greek: 'In this sign conquer'. He adopted this as his symbol – the labarum. In 325 he called the **Nicene Council** and this was the first great **Council** of the **Church**.

Consubstantiation the **Protestant** teaching about **Holy Communion** put forward by **Martin Luther** to counter the Roman Catholic **doctrine** of **transubstantiation**. It states that during the service, the **bread** becomes conjoined (united) with the body of Christ and the wine with the blood. Yet the bread remains bread and the wine remains wine.

Contemplation a way of approaching God through **prayer**. It is a stage beyond **meditation** and involves a total detachment from the world around to spend time in God's presence. Several monastic orders are 'contemplative' and their members follow this way of life.

Contraception also called birth control. This refers to all methods used to avoid starting a pregnancy (conception) after sexual intercourse has taken place. It is acceptable to most **Christians**. **Protestant Churches** accepted the idea that 'birth prevention', as it was called, was desirable after seeing the widespread poverty caused by the Depression of the 1930s. The **Roman Catholic Church**, however, has always expressed its opposition to all artificial means of birth control. An **encyclical** from the **Pope** in 1968, called **Humanae Vitae**, stated that all such artificial methods were against the will of God. Catholics, he declared, could only use '**natural family planning**' with a clear conscience.

Convent the building in which members of female religious orders (communities) live, although originally the word could be applied to male religious houses as well. Members of a convent are covered by the same **vows** as male orders – poverty, **chastity** and obedience. Convents are also often used as centres for educational and medical work.

Conversion in the Christian faith, this means turning from a life of **sin** and selfishness to one of serving God. Conversion may be sudden and dramatic, as in the case of St **Paul** on the Damascus road (Acts 9:1–9), or take place over a period of time. In

Evangelical churches the word is applied to a sudden realisation of **Christ** as Saviour.

Corpus Christi from the Latin phrase meaning 'the body of Christ', this feast in the **Roman Catholic Church** is held in honour of the presence of **Christ** in the **bread** and wine of the **Mass**. Corpus Christi was first celebrated in the 14th century and its main feature in many countries is a procession after **Mass** when the 'host' (the consecrated bread) is paraded in front of the people. The festival is celebrated on the Thursday following Trinity Sunday. ▶ See also **consecration**.

Corrymeela Community this was founded in Northern Ireland in 1965 by Protestant and Roman Catholic **Christians** at the height of the troubles there. Its main aim is to bring about the reconciliation (togetherness) of the two communities. People from both communities put aside their differences and talk and help each

> **CORRYMEELA**
> *IS*
> PEOPLE OF ALL AGES AND CHRISTIAN TRADITIONS WHO INDIVIDUALLY AND TOGETHER ARE COMMITTED TO THE HEALING OF SOCIAL, RELIGIOUS AND POLITICAL DIVISIONS THAT EXIST IN NORTHERN IRELAND AND THROUGHOUT THE WORLD.

A symbol of people coming together in a spirit of friendship.

other. They also worship and pray together at Corrymeela.

Council formal meetings of **bishops** where matters of **doctrine** or behaviour are discussed and decided upon. They have been important in the life of the **Roman Catholic Church** for centuries, being part of the **magisterium** (teaching ministry of the Church). Ecumenical Councils are of the whole Church and their statements carry the highest authority. There have been 21 in the history of the Catholic Church, of which the most recent was the **Second Vatican Council** from 1961 to 1965. This gave a new shape to the Catholic Church in the 20th century.

Counter-Reformation during the 16th century, the **Reformation**, led by **Martin Luther** and **John Calvin**, caused a break with **Rome** and resulted in the formation of the **Protestant Church**. At the same time a movement took place within the **Roman Catholic Church** to strengthen it, called the Counter-Reformation. New religious orders came into existence. The Council of Trent, which shaped the **Church** for the next 400 years, met from 1545 to 1563. This was one of the most important **Councils** in the history of the Catholic Church.

Cranmer,Thomas (1489–1556) the founder of the **Reformation** in England. He was appointed **Archbishop of Canterbury** by Henry VIII in 1532, when the king broke away from the **Pope** in **Rome**. Cranmer set up the **Church of England** and the **Book of Common Prayer**. He was finally burnt at the stake during the reign of Queen Mary.

Creed from the Latin meaning 'I believe', what is known as the Creed is a summary of the main aspects of Christian belief. From the beginning of the **Church**'s existence, brief creeds in the **New Testament** (e.g. 'Jesus is Lord') were used in **baptisms**. From these short statements, the **Apostles Creed** and **Nicene Creed** grew in later centuries. These appear on page 82.

Crib literally, a manger or container for animal food; used widely to mean a model representing the scene of **Christ**'s birth which is placed in many **churches** on Christmas Eve. The baby **Jesus**, his mother Mary, Joseph and various animals, are then placed in the crib. The figures of the **Magi** are added at **Epiphany**. St **Francis of Assisi** is thought to have made the first crib in 1223.

Crosier the staff carried by a **bishop** or **abbot** which is bent at the end like a shepherd's crook. This is a reminder that he is like a shepherd looking after his flock. As he walks in a procession, perhaps before a **confirmation**, the bishop turns his staff outwards to indicate his authority.

Cross usually an upright stake with a crossbeam, this was the method used by the Romans to execute all non-Roman criminals sentenced to death. Since the crucifixion (killing by fixing to a cross) of **Jesus** around 29 CE, the cross has become the main symbol of **Christianity**. Since the 2nd century, the **sign of the cross** has been used as both a sign of **faith** and a **blessing** and many **Christians** still use it today. ▶ See also **sign of the cross**.

Crucifix from the 5th century onwards, crosses were produced with the figure of **Christ** on them for use in **worship**. To begin with **Jesus** was represented on the **cross** as a

The crucifix is a reminder for many Christians of the suffering and death of Jesus.

king. It is only since the 13th century that a figure of a suffering Christ has been shown. Crucifixes are found in Catholic and some Anglican **churches** but not in **Nonconformist** ones. People often wear crucifixes around their necks, although this may be as much a fashion accessory as a statement of faith.

Crusades a series of military expeditions by Christian armies between 1095 and 1291. The aim was to take the Holy Land of **Israel** back from the Muslims and put Christian leaders in their place. The Crusaders also wanted to secure the right of Christian pilgrims to visit holy places in **Palestine**. The Crusades were financed by various **Popes** who promised a reward in the after-life for all those who died in the holy effort.

Curate at one time, a curate was a **priest** in charge of a **parish**. Now, however, it is the assistant priest working alongside a **vicar**. Most curates spend two spells of three years each in a parish before they become a vicar with a parish of their own.

Curia the entire organisation that helps the **Bishop of Rome**, the **Pope**, in the **Vatican** to carry out his duties. There are ten different offices in the Curia – covering such aspects of the **Roman Catholic Church**'s life as education, **evangelism**, **worship** and the **sacraments**.

Deacon There are three 'holy orders' in the **Roman Catholic, Anglican** and **Orthodox Churches – bishop, priest** and deacon. In the **New Testament**, deacons were administrators in the Christian community but in today's **Church** it is the first stage towards **ordination**. In the **Church of England**, they are able to take much of the responsibility in a **parish** but cannot celebrate the **Eucharist**. After twelve months, however, they can be ordained as a priest. In many **Free Churches**, most notably the **Baptist Church**, deacons are elected from the congregation to help the **minister** run the church.

Deaconess a woman ordained to assist in a **parish** and carry out religious work. The deaconess usually wears distinctive dress. In the early **Church**, deaconesses were chosen only from widows who were at least 40 years old. In 1994, women were ordained into the priesthood in the **Church of England** and the office stopped. It still exists, however, in some **Nonconformist** Churches.

Dead Sea the sea into which the River **Jordan** flows. The Dead Sea is about 46 miles long and between 5 and 9 miles wide. The water is some 1,200 feet below sea level. It is very unusual in that its salt content is about 25 per cent compared with the norm for seawater of between 3 per cent and 4 per cent.

Dead Sea Scrolls a group of ancient documents including manuscripts of the **Old Testament**. They were discovered by a Bedouin goatherd in a cave at the north east end of the **Dead Sea** in 1947. They came from the **monastery** of a Jewish sect called the **Essenes** and were written in **Hebrew** and **Aramic** between 150 BCE and 70 CE.

Dean an official in the **Roman Catholic** and **Anglican Churches**. In the Catholic Church, the dean is chosen by a **bishop** to supervise several **dioceses**. In the **Church of England**, a dean is the official who has charge of the care and upkeep of a **cathedral**.

Dedication of infants in the **Baptist Church, baptism** is reserved for adults. Babies are brought before the church congregation in a service of infant dedication. God is thanked for the safe delivery of the child and prayers are offered for the baby's future. The wish is expressed that the child might come to know **Jesus**

Christ as their personal Saviour. The parents state publicly their wish to bring the child up in line with the teachings of the **Bible**.

Demon in biblical times, a demon was an evil spirit. **Jesus** accepted their existence and is said to have delivered people from their power on more than one occasion (Mark 1:34, 39). **Paul** believed that such spirits were behind much of the opposition that he encountered (1. Corinthians 10:20–21).

Denomination a group of **churches** with the same name and similar beliefs. There are now hundreds of **Protestant** denominations, among them the **Church of England**, the **Baptists**, the **Methodists**, the **Salvation Army** and the **United Reformed Church**.

Devil presented in the **Bible** as the supreme force of evil. Also known as **Satan**, the Devil controls a whole army of lesser devils or **demons**. He began as one of God's leading **angels** but rebelled and was sent out of **heaven**. Confronting **Jesus** at the start of his **ministry** (Luke 4:1–13), the Devil was finally defeated when Jesus returned to life after his **resurrection** from the dead.

Diocese a geographical area of the **church** placed under the supervision of a **bishop**. Each diocese is divided up into **parishes** which are in the care of a **priest**. Several parishes are then grouped together under the leadership of an archdeacon.

Disciple meaning someone who learns or is a pupil. So, a Christian **disciple** is one who follows **Christ** and learns from him. **Jesus** chose twelve men to be his disciples and they remained with him to the end of his life. One of them, though, **Judas Iscariot**, betrayed him. ▶See also **Apostles**.

Dispensation special permission granted by the **Pope** to allow a Roman Catholic not to do something which their faith actually demands of them. Occasionally, for example, people have been given special permission to marry someone although the teaching of the **Church** forbids them to do so.

Divine Liturgy in the **Eastern Orthodox Church**, the most important service, the **Eucharist**, is known as the Divine Liturgy. A liturgy is the written service of church **worship**, usually found in a service or prayer book. In the **Anglican Church**, this can be the **Book of Common Prayer** or the **Alternative Service Book**. The **Roman Catholic** service book is called the **Missal**.

Divorce the legal dissolution (break-up) of a **marriage**. Christian wedding services state clearly that the marriage is for ever although some **Protestants** do accept divorce on the basis of Matthew 5:32, if **adultery** has taken place. The **Church of England** accepts divorce but most **vicars** will not remarry divorced people. The **Roman Catholic Church** does not recognise it.

Doctrine the teachings of the **Christian Church** in general or any **denomination** in particular. In the **Roman Catholic Church**, the main beliefs have been given by divine **revelation** to the **Church** and have been laid down through the centuries by **Popes** or **Church Councils**. When the Church recognises these beliefs they become dogmas and binding on all Catholics.

Dogma a **doctrine** which is taught by the **Church** so strongly that its members have to accept it.

Dominicans an order (community) of **friars** who are often called the Black Friars. The order was founded by St. Dominic at Toulouse, in France, in 1215 and its motto – *Veritas* (Latin for 'truth') – provides a clue to the kind of work it does. It is a teaching order with male preachers who spread the truth to others, whilst Dominican **nuns** spend their time in **prayer** and **contemplation**. St Dominic is always pictured with a sparrow by his side and a dog carrying a burning torch in his mouth.

Dormition of the Virgin from the Latin 'to sleep'. The festival celebrated by the **Orthodox Church** of the falling asleep of the **Virgin Mary** before she was taken into **heaven**. The equivalent in the **Roman Catholic Church** is the **Assumption of the Virgin Mary**, celebrated on August 15th.

Douai Bible a translation of the **Bible** by English Roman Catholics from the Latin **Vulgate** version. The **New Testament** was published in 1582 and the **Old Testament** in 1609. Both **translations** were published at Rheims and the full Bible is called the 'Douai and Rheims' version.

Dove used extensively in Christian art to symbolise the **Holy Spirit**, with the seven rays coming out of it representing the gifts of the Holy Spirit. The dove is often shown with the **Virgin Mary** at the **Annunciation**.

Doxology a **hymn** of praise to God which is addressed to the different members of the **Trinity**. It is sometimes sung at the end of hymns. The most common form that it takes is 'Glory be to the Father, and to the Son, and to the Holy Ghost (Spirit)'. The hymn 'Praise God from whom all blessings flow' is also known as the Doxology.

East as the sun rises in the east many **Christians** turn towards that direction as the **Creed** is being said, to express their belief that **Christ** is the 'Sun of Righteousness'. In traditional **churches** the **altar** is placed in front of the east wall to remind worshippers of the same thing. In the past people were often buried with their feet facing east to show that they died in the hope of being raised to life at the **Second Coming**.

Easter the name comes from the Old English word 'eastre'. This was a pagan festival held in honour of the goddess of dawn. Easter is the most important festival in the **Christian Church**, celebrated each year in March or April. The festival begins with **Good Friday**, when the death of **Jesus** is remembered, and ends on **Easter Day** when **Christians** celebrate the **resurrection** (rising) of Jesus from the dead.

Easter Day the most joyful occasion in the Christian year. It celebrates the **resurrection** of **Jesus** from the dead. Its importance is emphasised by the long time of preparation through **Lent** followed by the solemn services of **Holy Week**. Then follows **Easter Day** when

many **Christians** reply to the **priest**'s words, 'He is risen', with the response, 'He is risen indeed'. It was a common belief that the sun danced on Easter Days.

Eastern Orthodox Church a family of self-governing **Churches** found mainly in eastern Europe, especially the old Soviet Union and around the eastern Mediterranean. Each Church is led by a senior **bishop** called a **patriarch**, with special honour being given to the Patriarch of Constantinople. It claims to have an unbroken line of descent from the Church which **Christ** and his **Apostles** established. The Eastern Orthodox Church broke with the **Roman Catholic Church** in the **Great Schism** of 1054. ▶ See also **apostolic succession**.

Ecumenical Movement from the Greek meaning 'the whole inhabited world', this movement has led attempts to bring the various **Churches** closer together during the 20th century. In 1948, the **World Council of Churches** was formed and all the major Churches joined, with the exception of the **Roman Catholic Church**. As only a handful of small Churches have united this century, many people feel that the work of the Ecumenical Movement has not been particularly successful. ►See also **World Council of Churches**.

Elder in the **New Testament**, this was a senior figure in a **church**. Today, several **Free Churches** have elders who are responsible for teaching, taking part in discussions about running the church and its policy. They are often responsible for leading the social work of the church.

Elevation of the Host the raising of the **host** and the **chalice** in front of the people in the congregation which takes place during the **Mass**, after the **consecration**. This allows the people to adore the **body of Christ**.

Elim Pentecostal Church one of several Pentecostal Churches that came into existence in 1915. The Pentecostalists are a small group of **Christians** who believe in **'speaking in tongues'** and **prophecy**. ►See also **Pentecostal movement**.

Emmaus the village in which **Jesus** made an appearance to two of his **disciples** after his **resurrection** (Luke 24:13–35). They did not recognise him until he broke **bread** with them.

Encyclical a letter sent by the **Pope** in Latin to all the **cardinals** and **bishops** of the **Roman Catholic Church**. It concerns some teaching which the Pope wishes to be passed on to the members of the **Church** throughout the world.

Epiphany meaning 'manifestation' or 'showing'. In the Western **Church** this is the festival which comes soon after **Christmas** (January 6th) to commemorate the visit of the **Magi** or Wise Men to the baby **Jesus**. This visit was important because the Magi were the first non-Jews (**Gentiles**) to visit Jesus. For members of the **Eastern Orthodox Church**, however, Epiphany commemorates the **baptism** of Jesus by **John the Baptist**.

Episcopacy the system of **Church** government which places a **bishop** in charge of a **diocese**. The **Roman Catholic Church**, the **Anglican Church** and the **Orthodox Church** are all episcopal. They believe that their bishops are descended directly from those bishops who had a similar ministry in the early Church. ►See also **apostolic succession, bishop**.

Epistle a letter. In the **New Testament** there are many letters written by such early **Church** leaders as **Paul, Peter**, James and **John**. Most of these epistles were written to pass on some **doctrine** or teaching, either to individual **Christians** or to whole Christian communities. Paul, for instance, wrote two letters to Timothy, a young church leader, and a long epistle to the Christians in Rome. Peter sent two letters and John three.

Eschatology this word meaning 'last things' refers to the teaching in the **Bible** of what will happen when God brings the world to an end. It concerns the end of the present age, the **Second Coming** of **Christ** to the earth, the **Last Judgement, heaven** and **hell**.

Essenes a Jewish religious group which began living along the edge of the **Dead Sea** in the 2nd century BCE. They kept the **Sabbath Day** very strictly. It is possible that **John the Baptist** spent some time with them. In some ways their way of life was similar to that of **Jesus** and his disciples. ▶ See also **Dead Sea Scrolls**.

Established Church in England, the **Church of England** is the Established Church, having had a close link with the State since the time of Henry VIII. This means that the Queen is its head, and that the Prime Minister appoints the **archbishops** and **bishops**. Bishops from the Church of England sit in the House of Lords – a privilege which no other **Church** enjoys. The **Archbishop of Canterbury** leads the service on great State occasions like a coronation or the funeral of a monarch.

Eternal life a term used in **John's Gospel** to describe membership of the **Kingdom of God**. Eternal life is enjoyed by people on earth when they have a relationship with God through **Jesus Christ**. It continues after death when they go to **heaven** and live in God's presence forever.

Eternal punishment the **New Testament** says that everyone will appear before God at the **Last Judgement**. He will judge them and those guilty of rejecting God's love during their life on earth will be sentenced to eternal (everlasting) punishment in **hell**.

Eucharist taken from the Greek word meaning 'thanksgiving', this is one of several terms used for the central service in most **Churches**. It is also called **Holy Communion**. The Eucharist is particularly important since, along with **baptism**, it is one of the two **sacraments** which **Jesus** specifically told his followers they must celebrate. The **Quakers** and the **Salvation Army** are the only two mainstream Christian **denominations** which do not celebrate it.

Eucharistic prayer the most important part of the Catholic service of the **Mass**. In this **prayer**, thanks is given to God for the sacrifice of **Christ** on the **cross**. The **bread** and wine are also consecrated to God and these shortly become the body and blood of **Jesus**. ▶ See also **consecration**.

Eucharistic vestments items of clothing worn by a **priest** while celebrating the **Eucharist**. In most **churches** six different vestments are worn during this service.

Euthanasia meaning 'easy death', this is the early ending of a person's life to save them from unnecessary pain and suffering. Euthanasia is a fiercely debated issue in the Christian community, as it is in society generally. Many people believe that it is right to end a person's life, with their consent, if they have an illness for which there is no cure. At the moment it is illegal in almost every country. All the **Churches**, however, oppose it because they believe that God alone has the right to decide when someone should die.

Evangelicals **Christians** of any **Protestant denomination** who believe that **a** the **Bible** is the inspired Word of God and without error. **b** an individual can only become a **Christian** by repenting of his or her **sins** and turning to Christ in **faith**. **c** all Christians have the responsibility to share the **Gospel** or 'Good News' with those who are not yet 'saved'. This activity is called **evangelism**. In the **Church of England**, Evangelicals are often known as '**Low Church**'.

Evangelism the practice of spreading the 'Good News' of **salvation** through the death and **resurrection** of **Jesus**. The aim is to persuade people to accept Jesus Christ as their personal saviour. Once a person is converted to **Christ** in an Evangelical church they must take some part in evangelism. This goes on in church, in large meetings, on street corners and through one-to-one conversations. ▶ See also **Evangelicals**.

Evening Prayer the evening service in Anglican **churches** and the equivalent of Roman Catholic Vespers. The old name for this is Evensong. It usually includes **hymns**, **psalms**, **Bible** readings, the **Apostles Creed** (see p. 82), **prayers** and a **sermon**.

Ex cathedra meaning 'from the chair'. This refers to what the **Pope** says when he is speaking from his **bishop**'s chair or papal throne in his official capacity as the Vicar of Christ on earth. Anything that the Pope says ex cathedra is believed to be infallible and so binding on all Roman Catholics. ▶ See also **infallibility**.

Excommunication when someone is excluded from the fellowship and **worship** of a **Church**. The **Roman Catholic Church** is the only one that still uses excommunication occasionally as a form of punishment, when the **Pope** considers that a person has placed themselves outside the Church by what they have said or done. The person involved is usually a leader or someone who has real influence over other people. If the person is ordained they cannot continue to administer the **sacraments**.

Exodus **1** one of the books of the **Old Testament**. **2** when **Moses** led the Israelites out of slavery in Egypt to the verge of the Promised Land (Canaan), now known as **Israel**. The journey took 40 years.

Exorcism the driving out of evil spirits or **demons** from a person or a place. **Jesus** and his **Apostles** used exorcism on more than one occasion – Matthew 10:1ff; Acts 16:18. It is rarely practised today except in such **denominations** as the Pentecostalists.

Extreme unction the old name for the practice of **anointing** the sick – one of the seven **sacraments** of the **Roman Catholic Church**. In the past it was only given to people expected to die and so was called 'extreme'. Now it is extended to those who expect to be healed by God as well. The practice is based upon James 5.14: 'Is there any sick among you? let him call for the elders of the church; and let them pray over him, anointing him with oil in the name of the Lord.'

F

Faith There are two aspects to faith, or belief, within the **Christian Church**: **1** those who belong to the Christian Church must believe certain 'truths' – that God exists, that God is love etc. These beliefs are called 'the Faith of the Church'. **2** those who are Christians must accept their own sinfulness and their need for forgiveness by God. That forgiveness can only be accepted by faith in God. It comes freely as a gift from God through **Jesus Christ**.

Fall according to the Book of Genesis in the **Old Testament**, God made the first man and the first woman and placed them both in the Garden of Eden. He told them that they could eat any fruit from the garden – apart from the fruit of the tree of the knowledge of good and evil. The tempting voice of a serpent (snake), however, did persuade them to eat and so the first **sin** was committed. According to **Paul** in the **New Testament**, this sin has affected the whole of mankind since all people are now born sinful. The sin of the man and woman, therefore, was a fall from a state of goodness to one of sinfulness.

Fasting either a total or a partial abstinence from (giving up of) food for a certain period of time. In the past, fasting was a popular spiritual exercise amongst **Christians**. Its aim was to heighten a person's self discipline and spiritual awareness. It was particularly associated with **Lent**. Although fasting has largely died out in most **Churches**, it is still kept alive in a few religious orders. ▶ See also **abstinence**.

Father the favourite name of **Jesus** for God. In the Christian **faith**, God is a **Trinity** with one member being God the Father. The name is also used in the **Roman Catholic Church** for a **priest**, as it is by **High Church Anglicans**.

Fatima a small town in Portugal which has become famous as a place of **pilgrimage**. In 1917, three young children saw visions of a woman who said that she was Our Lady of the Rosary (the **Virgin Mary**). She told the children to say the **rosary** each day and build a church in her honour.

Feasts of obligation in the **Roman Catholic Church**, there are many festivals (feasts) which are very important, when all **priests** must say **Mass**. Ordinary church members must attend Mass on these days.

Fish used as a symbol of **Christ** by the early **Christians** because the letters of its Greek name (*icthus*) formed an acronym with the initial letters of the words 'Jesus Christ, Son of God and Saviour' in Greek. On days of **abstinence** in the **Roman Catholic Church**, fish takes the place of meat.

Font meaning a 'spring of water', this is a stone container which is

used to hold the water for **infant baptism**. Traditionally, the font has been placed just inside the door of a **church** – as a symbol of the belief that **baptism** is the door into Church membership. In modern churches, the font is sometimes placed in the middle of the congregation to indicate that the church community promises to love and care for the baby as it grows up.

Fornication the word used in the **Bible** (Galatians 5:19; Ephesians 5:3) for sexual intercourse between two unmarried people.

Fox, George (1624–91) founded the Society of Friends (**Quakers**). In 1647, Fox left the **Church** and began to preach that the 'inner voice of God' speaks to the soul. Fox refused to take up weapons or to take his hat off to anyone. Although often in prison, he began to attract many followers and the Quaker movement grew.

Francis of Assisi, Saint (1182–1226) in 1205, he turned to a life of **prayer** and poverty and founded the **Franciscan** religious order in 1209. After leading the movement for a while, he retired to live a life of solitude for his last three years. His begging **friars** lived in extreme poverty. Francis has become a symbol for a simple life; devotion to God and his fellow man and a passionate love of nature. He was made a **saint** (canonised) two years after his death, in 1228.

Franciscans a Roman Catholic and an Anglican religious order founded by **St Francis of Assisi** in 1209. Its **friars**, who have no possessions, follow the example of St Francis, who lived a life in harmony with God and nature.

Free Churches those **Nonconformist Churches** which do not owe any allegiance to the **Anglican** or **Roman Catholic Churches**. These include the **Baptist** and **Methodist Churches**. They are so-called because they are 'free' of any link with the state.

Friar a **monk** in the **Roman Catholic** or **Anglican Church** who does not live all the time in one community. He is free to move from one to another within his order.

Friars take a vow of poverty when they join their order and combine work outside the community – usually medical or social work – with a life of **prayer**.

Friend a **Quaker**, a member of the Society of Friends.

Fundamentalism a movement within the **Protestant Church** which began early in the 20th century. It teaches that the **Bible** is never wrong (infallible) since every word in it was made known by God to those who wrote it down. The writers were little more than secretaries recording the thoughts of God. Fundamentalists have always strongly opposed evolution and accepted the literal truth of the story of creation in the Book of Genesis.

Galilee at the time of the **New Testament**, Galilee meant all the area of north **Palestine** from the Mediterranean Sea to the River **Jordan**. Nearly all of **Christ**'s early life and much of his teaching took place here. **Jesus** was called 'the Galilean'. The word was also applied to his followers.

Gehenna a valley to the south of **Jerusalem**. **Jews** had always looked upon it as the place where God punished those who had not been true to the Jewish faith. The early **Christians** believed it was the final place of rest for those condemned to **hell** at the **Last Judgement**.

General Synod the central decision-making body of the **Church of England**. Until 1969, it was known as the Church Assembly. There are three parts or 'houses' to the General Synod – **bishops**, **clergy** and **laity**. All bishops automatically belong to the Synod whilst the other members are elected. Important changes in the Church of England need to receive more than 66 per cent of the vote in all three houses before they are debated by Parliament.

Gentile in the **Bible**, a Gentile is anyone who is not a **Jew**. The word was particularly applied to **Christians**.

Genuflection a practice followed mainly in the **Roman Catholic** and **High Church** as a way of expressing respect for God. The right knee is bent to touch the ground, often while the person is bowing. People genuflect when they pass in front of the **reserved sacrament** on the **altar**, as they enter or leave a **church**, or when the **Pope**, a **cardinal** or a **bishop** passes in front of them.

Gethsemane a small garden just outside **Jerusalem**. The traditional location is the Mount of Olives, east of the ravine of Kidron. After sharing the **Last Supper** with his

disciples, **Jesus** took three of them – **Peter**, James and **John** – with him to Gethsemane. It was here that Jesus prayed that God would stop him having to go through the agony of his forthcoming death.

Gideons an international association of Christian businessmen who seek to introduce others to **Christianity** by leaving **Bibles** in such places as hotels, airports, dentists' waiting-rooms etc. There are now Gideons in more than 60 different countries.

Glossolalia the practice, which has become widespread in some branches of the **Church**, of **'speaking in tongues'**. Many **Christians** believe this to be a gift of the **Holy Spirit**. It is used to **worship** God, to pray and to communicate some word of **prophecy** or vision from God. The gift is particularly emphasised by members of the **Pentecostalist** and **Charismatic movements**.

Godparents godfathers and godmothers are adults who assume responsibility for the spiritual welfare of a baby at his or her **baptism**. They also promise to turn away from evil and to help bring the child up in a Christian way. They accept this responsibility until the child goes forward for **confirmation**.

Golgotha the **Hebrew** word for **Calvary**, the place outside the city of

Jerusalem where **Jesus** was crucified. It means 'skull' on account of the shape of the rock.

Good Friday the day on which **Christians** throughout the world remember the death of **Jesus** on a **cross** at **Calvary**. On this day **churches** are stripped bare of everything except the basic furniture. In the **Roman Catholic Church**, there is a service of **prayers** and **Bible** readings before the **Veneration of the Cross** at 3 pm – the time that Jesus is believed to have died. In the **Anglican Church**, there is often a three-hour service from noon to 3 pm.

Good News Bible a modern illustrated version of the **Bible** produced by the American Bible Society. First called *Today's English Version*, the **New Testament** translation was published in 1966. The complete Bible followed in 1976.

Gospel meaning 'Good News' in Greek. The 'Good News' for **Christians** is that God has kept his promises and opened up a way of forgiveness through the death and **resurrection** of **Jesus**. This message stands at the centre of the life and **faith** of the **Church**.

Gospels there are four Gospels in the **New Testament – Matthew**, **Mark**, **Luke** and **John**. They all give descriptions of the way **Jesus** served God, his life, death and **resurrection**. The first three present a similar picture of **Jesus** and so they are called the **Synoptic Gospels**, from the word meaning 'seeing together'. The fourth Gospel, John's presents a very different picture.

Graham, Billy an American evangelist, born in 1918, who has preached to more people than anyone else in history. He conducts 'Crusades' (large meetings) throughout the world and first came to Britain in 1954.

Great Schism from the 5th century, the **Churches** in the West and those in the East disagreed over the power of the **Pope**. In 1054, the break between the two Churches became permanent. The Church in the West accepted the authority of the Pope and became the **Roman Catholic Church**. The Church in the East, which rejected the Pope's authority, developed into the **Eastern Orthodox Church**. The two Churches remain separate today.

Habit the distinctive clothing of religious orders worn by **nuns**, **monks** and **friars**. Since the **Second Vatican Council**, members of these orders have been able to wear ordinary clothes instead – and many have chosen to do so.

Hail Mary the translation of the first two words of the Latin prayer to the **Virgin Mary** also known as the **Ave Maria**, used in the **Roman Catholic Church**. The phrase is applied to the smaller beads of a **rosary**. See Appendix on page 83.

Halo in Christian art, a halo is a circle of light painted around the head to show that a person is thought to be particularly holy. To begin with, it was used only on paintings of **Jesus** but was then extended to the **Virgin Mary** and other **saints**. The **Roman Catholic Church** only allows a halo to be placed around the head of someone who has been canonised or beatified. ►See also **beatification, canonisation**.

Harvest Festival a comparatively new Christian festival, only dating from the middle of the 19th century, although several much older agricultural festivals were celebrated before this. For Harvest, people bring the produce of the land to decorate the **church** and thank God for yet another good harvest. The goods are then given away to the poor and the needy in the area.

Healing the curing of bodily and mental illness by the power of God. **Jesus** and his **disciples** healed the sick (Matthew 10:1; Acts 3:1–11), whilst **Christians** were told to pray for healing (James 5:14–16). The **sacrament** of healing, often called **extreme unction**, is used regularly by the **Roman Catholic Church**.

Heaven in the **Bible**, heaven is the place where God and his **angels** live – and the final resting place for all those who place their trust in God on earth. As nobody knows what heaven is like it can only be imagined, but believers see it as a city of gold in which the faithful **Christian** enjoys the continued **blessing** of God.

Hebrew the language in which almost all of the **Old Testament** was written. This ancient language runs from right to left on the page. The original text was written in consonants only. Vowels (a series of dots and dashes) were added much later.

Hebrews 1 the earliest people in the **Bible** from **Abraham** onwards were known as Hebrews. They usually spoke of themselves as Israelites. **2** one of the **epistles** in the **New Testament**. For a long time **Paul** was thought to be the writer but it is now known to be anonymous.

Hell the opposite of **heaven**. It is a place of everlasting torment and punishment (Matthew 25:46). After death, people go to hell who have lived lives on earth without **faith** in God. The early **Christians** associated it with the place they knew as **Gehenna** meaning 'the Valley of the Hinnom'. At the time of **Jesus**, this was a rubbish dump with fires continually burning.

Heresy a **doctrine** or belief which is chosen in place of the official teaching of the **Church**. A heretic is someone who deliberately holds these views. Although the Church rarely speaks out against heresy today, it has, in the past, condemned many who disagreed with the Church's teaching on such matters as the **Trinity** and the Person of **Christ**, and expelled them from the Church.

Hermit someone who withdraws from the world and its pleasures, usually for religious reasons. He also withdraws from the company of other people and lives a life of solitude, often in a desert area. There are few hermits today, although some do remain in the **Eastern Orthodox Church**.

Herod the Great (70–4 BCE) he was given the task of ruling over Judea by Octavian and Antony in 40 BCE and he did so with great brutality. Although he rebuilt the Jewish **Temple** in **Jerusalem**, he was hated by his Jewish subjects. In the last year of Herod's rule, **Jesus** was born. Herod, who had heard that a king had been born who would rival him, tried to kill him by putting to death all male babies under the age of two in Jerusalem (Matthew 2.16). This event is remembered by some **churches** on December 28th as the festival of the Holy Innocents.

High altar the main **altar** in a **church**. It is usually to be found in front of the east wall.

High Church those members of the **Church of England** whose beliefs and ways of worshipping are closest to the **Roman Catholic Church**. Also known as **Anglo-Catholics**, these **Christians** emphasise the importance of **Church** tradition, the **sacraments** and the place of **bishops**. Most of the High Church were strongly against the decision to ordain women which was taken by the **Church of England** in 1992. Some even left the **Anglican Communion** and joined the Roman

Catholic Church as a result. ▶ See also **ordination, ordination of women**.

High Mass **Mass** is the most important service in the **Roman Catholic Church**. A High Mass is one in which the celebrant, **bishop** or **priest**, is assisted by a **deacon** together with a **choir** and other acolytes. **Incense** is freely used. It is usually celebrated on an important feast day or special occasion.

High Priest an old office in the Jewish religion, going all the way back to Aaron, the brother of **Moses** (Exodus 28). The High Priest wore a special breastplate and mitre. He alone was able to enter the Holy of Holies in the **Temple**, the place where God was believed to dwell. At the time of the death of **Jesus**, the High Priest was **Caiaphas**. The office no longer exists.

Holocaust an offering, or sacrifice, which is totally consumed by fire, making it a perfect offering. Since the Second World War, it has been used to refer to the six million **Jews** who were slaughtered in concentration camps by the Nazis.

Holy Communion **1** the whole church service otherwise known as the **Eucharist**. **2** the receiving of the **bread** and wine during the Eucharist service. This act is one of 'holy communion' (fellowship) between God and the worshipper. In the **Anglican Church**, the **clergy** and the

laity receive both the bread and wine. In the **Roman Catholic Church**, however, the clergy receive both, but the laity only the bread.

Holy Orders in the **Roman Catholic** and **Orthodox Churches** there are three holy orders – **bishop**, **priest** and **deacon**. Men become members of these orders through the **sacrament** of **ordination** which is always carried out by a bishop. All priests are required to celebrate **Mass** every day. Although the **Anglican Church** does not regard ordination as a sacrament, all bishops, priests and deacons are ordained. When a person is ordained he or she is said to 'take holy orders'. ▶ See also **ordination, ordination of women**.

Holy Saturday the last day of **Lent**: the day between **Good Friday** and **Easter** in **Holy Week**. **Churches** are often cleaned on this day as **Christians** remember the time that **Jesus** was buried in a borrowed tomb after he had been crucified.

Holy Scriptures those books which make up the **Bible**. Most **Churches** accept that they carry a special authority since they contain everything that a **Christian** needs to know for his or her **salvation**.

Holy Spirit in Christian belief the Holy Spirit, or Holy Ghost, is the third person in the **Trinity**, being one God with God the Father and God the Son. In the **New Testament**, he is closely associated with **Jesus** and the work that he came to do. After Jesus left the earth, the Holy Spirit visited the first **Christians** on the Day of **Pentecost** and has come ever since to all those who believe in Jesus. ▶ See also **dove, Trinity**.

Holy water water which has been blessed and set aside for holy purposes. It is used, particularly in the **Roman Catholic** and **Orthodox Churches**, for such services as **baptism** and dedication and as a symbol of cleansing on entering a **church**.

Holy Week the last week of **Lent**, leading up to **Easter Day**. It begins with **Palm Sunday** and also includes **Maundy Thursday, Good Friday** and **Holy Saturday**. In the past it was used as a time for fasting before **Easter** and is still a time for special services in **church** in preparation for the great festival.

Homily a religious speech or **sermon** given by a **priest** or **minister** in a church service to members of the congregation. It usually explains the meaning of a passage from the **Bible**. Whilst it is called a **sermon** in most **Churches**, Roman Catholics prefer to use the word homily.

Homosexuality any form of sexual attraction and activity which draws together members of the same sex. (Heterosexuality refers to sexual attraction and behaviour involving members of the opposite sex.) The **Bible** and the **Church** have always condemned homosexual behaviour, with the **Roman Catholic Church** calling it 'unnatural'. The **Church of England**, however, has drawn a distinction between homosexual feelings, which it can accept, and homosexual behaviour, which it cannot support.

Hosanna the Greek form of an old **Hebrew prayer**. It means: 'Save us, Lord, we beseech thee.'

Host the **bread** used in **Holy Communion**. Its name comes from the Latin for a sacrificial victim because in the traditional Latin service it was believed to be the body of **Christ**, the victim on the **cross**. This thin wafer is used in most Anglican and all Roman Catholic **Eucharist** services. ▶ See also **Elevation of the Host**.

House-Church movement during the 1970s and 1980s, many groups of **Christians** left the established **Churches** to form small communities of their own. To begin with, these communities met in each other's houses (hence the name House-Church movement) although many of them later moved into larger premises. About 20,000 people now **worship** each **Sunday** in churches which belong to this movement. They place a great emphasis upon **music, speaking in tongues** and **prophecy**.

Humanae Vitae a famous **encyclical** (teaching document) issued by Pope Paul VI in 1968. In it all artificial means of birth control were condemned as 'unnatural' and against the will of God. Only **'natural family planning'** was allowed for Roman Catholics. ▶See also **contraception**.

Hymn a song of praise to God. Throughout the history of the **Christian Church**, hymns (poetry set to music) have been an essential part of **worship**. Some have been taken directly from the **Bible**, such as the **Psalms** and the songs in Luke 1. Since the 18th century, however, people such as Isaac Watts and Charles Wesley have written a great number of hymns, many of which are still sung today.

Icon a holy picture which is used as an aid to **worship** in the **Orthodox Church**, representing **Jesus Christ**, the **Virgin Mary** or a **saint** – or a combination of them. Traditionally, icons are painted on wood by highly trained painters using egg tempera.

Iconostasis in an **Orthodox Church**, a screen that separates the **sanctuary** from the main part of the **church** where the people sit. This screen is covered with five or more rows of **icons**. It has three doors with the central one called the Royal Door. This shuts off the **altar** (**sanctuary**) where the **Eucharist** is celebrated, in the holy presence of

Orthodox churches often contain many beautiful icons.

God, from the gaze of the people. Only the **priest** is allowed to pass through the iconostasis.

Immaculate Conception the
Roman Catholic belief that the **Virgin Mary**, the mother of **Jesus**, was conceived and born without **original sin**. This makes her different from every other human being except Jesus himself. In 1854, the **Pope** announced that Mary had lived her whole life without being tainted by sin and this has since become part of Roman Catholic belief. The feast of the Immaculate Conception is held on December 8th.

Immortality life which is endless.
In one sense the word can only be applied to God – who alone has neither beginning nor end. **Christians**, though, believe that they can now share in this endless life of God through the **resurrection** of **Jesus**.

Incarnation Christians believe
that **Jesus** is the eternal Son of God. Yet he was born as a human being in a stable in **Bethlehem**. He was born to the **Virgin Mary** and received from her his human nature. The mystery of how this happened is called the Incarnation. **Christians** believe that Jesus Christ was totally God and yet totally man.

Incense a sweet-smelling gum or
spice which lets off an odour when it is burned. Although it is used in most religions it means something special to some **Christians**. It represents **prayers** that are making their way slowly to **heaven**. It is an important feature of services in **Roman Catholic**, **Orthodox** and **Anglo-Catholic churches**.

Indulgence Roman Catholics
believe that the time a **soul** spends in **purgatory**, the place between **heaven** and **hell**, may be shortened by someone else undertaking good deeds (acts of merit) called indulgences on their behalf. In the Middle Ages, the practice was misused and became simply a way of raising money. When a special indulgence to finance the rebuilding of St Peter's Church in Rome was on sale, **Martin Luther** protested and this led to the **Protestant Reformation**.

Infallibility when a person cannot
make a mistake. If a **Pope** wishes to state a belief or **doctrine** which every Catholic must accept, he speaks **ex cathedra** and is never wrong (infallible). This means that he is safeguarded from making any error in what he says. Fundamentalist **Evangelicals** also speak of the **Bible** as infallible.

Infant baptism an important
sacrament in most of the major **Christian Churches** –including **Anglican**, **Roman Catholic** and **Orthodox**. In the ceremony the baby is sprinkled with water by a **priest** who also makes the **sign of the cross** on its forehead. Through

infant baptism, a child is welcomed into the Christian Church. ▶ See also **baptism, initiation**.

Initiation the means of entry into **Church** membership. For most **Christian Churches** this is through **baptism** – either as a baby or as an adult, as in the **Baptist Church**. Often the ceremony of initiation is reinforced by another ceremony which follows it. **Infant baptism**, for instance, is followed by **confirmation** some years later. **Adult baptism** in the Baptist Church is followed by the **minister** extending the 'right hand of fellowship' (a handshake) to the new member.

Inspiration of the Bible there are two ways the **Bible** can be seen as inspired or influenced by God: **1 Fundamentalist Christians** believe that the **Holy Spirit** so guided the authors of the different books in the Bible that they wrote what God wanted them to write. It is not possible, therefore, that the Bible should contain mistakes. **2** God 'breathes' into the words of the Bible so that they can come alive to each reader. There are mistakes in the Bible but they do not destroy its message.

Intercession praying on behalf of someone else. This can refer to two different things: **1** when a **Christian** prays to God for someone else. **2** when a Christian prays to **Jesus**, the **Virgin Mary** or one of the **saints** to plead with God on their behalf.

Iona a small island in the Inner Hebrides, off the coast of Scotland. St Columba founded a **monastery** there in 563. In the 1930s, George Macleod, with some helpers, began to rebuild the **abbey** on Iona and a religious community was formed. Its members, who spend a week on the island every year, are committed to regular **Bible**-reading, **prayer** and tithing (giving a tenth of their income to God's work).

Israel originally, this was the name given to Jacob after he wrestled with a stranger (Genesis 32:28). The name was then given to the ten tribes that were descended from his sons. Later these tribes united with two tribes of Judah to form the kingdom of Israel. This kingdom broke up in 722 BCE but the name survived on to describe the religious communities of **Jews** which were now scattered far and wide. In 1948, the country of Israel was brought into existence to provide a homeland for the Jews although many continue to live outside the country.

Jerusalem this city is very important to three different religions – **Christianity, Judaism** and Islam. It was first captured by King David in the **Old Testament** and his son, Solomon, built a beautiful **Temple** there. It was in Jerusalem that **Jesus** was crucified. The city today contains many places that are sacred to **Christians, Jews** and Muslims.

Jerusalem Bible a translation of the **Bible** by Roman Catholic scholars from original manuscripts into modern English. First published in 1966, this translation has been widely used in the **Roman Catholic Church** ever since.

Jesuit member of the Society of Jesus, a Roman Catholic religious order founded by St Ignatius Loyola in 1540. The Jesuits take **vows** of poverty, **chastity** and absolute obedience to any orders issued by the **Pope**. Today they carry out a

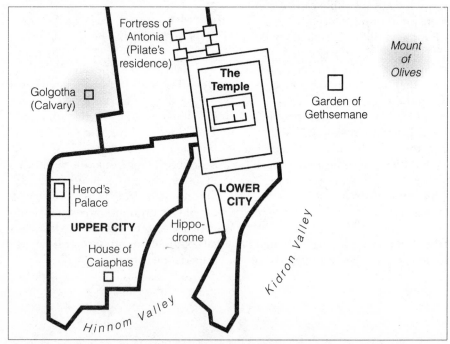

The holy city of Jerusalem, very important to Christians, Muslims and Jews alike.

wide variety of work throughout the world, mainly connected with education.

Jesus Christ Jesus is a Greek form of the name Joshua meaning, 'The Lord is salvation'. He was given the title Christ (**Messiah**) when people realised that he was fulfilling all the **prophecies** in the **Old Testament** which had looked forward to the coming of the Messiah. Jesus received his name from God the Father on the command of the **angel** who appeared to Joseph, his father: '… you shall give him the name Jesus, for he will save his people from their sins' (Matthew 1:21).

Jesus Prayer also known as the '**prayer** of the heart'. From the 6th century onwards **monks** and laypeople in the **Orthodox Church** have been using this prayer: 'Lord Jesus Christ, Son of God, have mercy on me.' It combines the worship of **Jesus**, a sorrow for one's own **sin** and confidence in the power of Jesus to forgive.

Jew a descendant of the Israelites in the **Old Testament** whose father, in a religious sense, is **Abraham**. According to Jewish law, a person is a Jew if he or she has a Jewish mother.

John John was the son of Zebedee and one of the original **disciples** of **Jesus**, along with his brother, James. His name has also been associated with one **Gospel** and three **Epistles**

in the **New Testament**, although we cannot be sure that we are speaking about the same John in each case. He is also believed to have written the book of the Revelation, the last book in the New Testament.

John the Baptist the cousin of **Jesus** and born to Elizabeth and Zachariah when they were both old. At an early age John went into the wilderness and lived on a diet of locusts and wild honey. His preaching prepared the people for the **ministry** of Jesus. This angered the authorities and after baptising Jesus in the River **Jordan**, John was finally arrested and beheaded by **Herod the Great**.

Jordan the river flowing through **Israel**. Four streams empty their water into the River Jordan. It then flows through the Lake of Galilee and into the **Dead Sea**. The Dead Sea is 1200 feet below sea-level – the lowest point above ground anywhere in the world. Much of **Jesus' ministry** took place on the banks of the River Jordan. It was there that he was baptised by **John the Baptist**.

Joseph husband of the **Virgin Mary** and the lawful father of **Jesus**. Joseph was a carpenter and Jesus worked with him until he went into public life when he was thirty years old. Tradition teaches that Joseph died soon after Jesus was born as he makes an early exit from the **Gospel** story.

Judaism the **faith** and religious practice of the Jewish people. All **Jews** trace their origins back to the early chapters of the **Bible** when **Abraham** was called by God to be the father of a mighty number of descendants – even though, at the time, he was childless and very old. Jews believe that they are God's Chosen People and so it is a faith into which people have to be born. Conversions to Judaism are very rare.

Judas Iscariot one of the original twelve **disciples** and the treasurer for the group. He betrayed **Jesus** to the Roman authorities for thirty pieces of silver with a kiss and afterwards committed suicide.

Judgement Day most **Christians** believe that at the end of the world, **Christ** will return on Judgement Day to judge the whole human race. It is then that those who have led good lives will be sent to **heaven**, whilst those who have been wicked will be sent to **hell** for ever.

Justification when a sinner is judged by God and yet receives forgiveness. **Protestants** believe that someone can only be justified through their **faith** in Christ. This belief is known as 'justification by faith' and was the key-note of the **Reformation**. The **Roman Catholic Church** teaches that faith and God's grace (goodness and mercy) through the **sacraments** are both important.

K

King James Version ▶ See **Authorised Version**.

King, Martin Luther (1929–68) the leader of the American Civil Rights Movement, which was dedicated to obtaining equal rights for black and white people. King was a **Baptist minister** and organised many forms of non-violent protest against prejudice and discrimination – including bus and café boycotts, and freedom marches. His life was ended by a bullet from the gun of a white assassin in Memphis, Tennessee.

Kingdom of God this phrase often occurs in the teaching of **Jesus** and is the theme of many of his **parables**. It has two meanings: **1** in this life the rule of God in the hearts and minds of men and women. **2** the age to come, when God will rule over everyone in **heaven** and they will obey him perfectly.

Kiss of peace this has been introduced recently into Anglican and Roman Catholic **worship**. It is the greeting of one another with a kiss or handshake as a sign of

Christian fellowship, as part of the **Eucharist** service.

Kneeling the usual position taken up by **Christians** when they are praying. Some **Churches**, though, encourage people to sit or stand instead. In the **Roman Catholic** and **Anglican Churches**, worshippers kneel when they receive the **sacrament** at the **Eucharist**.

Laity those baptised members of a Christian congregation who are neither ordained nor members of a religious order. In the **Roman Catholic Church**, the role of the laity in **church worship** was greatly increased by the **Second Vatican Council**. It emphasised that both laity and **clergy** are involved together in the work of spreading the **Gospel**. Every member of the Church has the responsibility to spread the good news of **Jesus** of

Nazareth by the way they carry out their daily lives.

Lamb of God an important Christian symbol. In **John**'s **Gospel**, the title 'Lamb of God' was given to **Jesus** (John 1:29). The lamb was an animal that was often used in sacrifice to symbolise purity and innocence. Applied to Jesus, this name drew attention to the purity and innocence of the one who died on the **cross** bearing the **sins** of the world. As a symbol for Jesus the title is often used in the **Eucharist**.

Lambeth Conference a gathering of **bishops** from the world-wide **Anglican Communion**. It takes place every ten years in the palace of the **Archbishop of Canterbury** in Lambeth. First held in 1867, the Conference discusses matters relating to the **Anglican Church** throughout the world.

Lammas Day an old Christian festival which is still celebrated by the **Roman Catholic Church** on August 1st. The name comes from the two words 'loaf' and 'mass' referring to the **bread** which was made from the first corn of the harvest and used during the **Mass** on this day. It also recalls the release of **Peter** from prison.

Last Day the final day of the present order of things. The day on which Christ, with his **angels**, returns to the earth for the final judgement of all human beings.
▶See also **Judgement Day.**

Last Supper the final meal that **Jesus** ate with his **disciples** shortly before he was arrested. He followed it by washing the feet of his disciples. St **Paul** calls this the **Lord's Supper** (1. Corinthians 11:20).

Last things ▶See **Eschatology.**

Laying on of hands in several **Church** services – **healing,**

confirmation and **ordination** – hands of one or more people are laid on the head of a person. This practice can be found in both the **Old Testament** (Numbers 27:18) and the **New Testament** (Acts 6:1–6). Although its exact meaning varies from service to service, it usually means the passing of some **blessing** to the person. In the case of ordination, authority is transferred and in confirmation, the **Holy Spirit** is passed to the person being confirmed.

Lectern a raised reading desk or moveable stand made of brass which holds the **Bible** in a **church**. There is usually a carving of an eagle supporting the stand symbolising St **John** and the inspiration of the **Gospels**. Anyone who is called up during a service to read from the Bible usually stands behind the lectern.

Lectionary an ordered system of **Bible** readings which shows the passages to be read at various **church** services throughout the **Church Year**. Different **churches** use different lectionaries and sometimes a Church has more than one. Lectionaries are used to make sure that as much of the Bible as possible is read throughout the year.

Lent an important season in the **Church Year**, beginning on **Ash Wednesday** and finishing on **Holy Saturday**. As a preparation for **Easter**, the celebration of **Christ's** death and **resurrection**, Lent is traditionally a time for **fasting** and **prayer**. The model for this is the 40 days that **Jesus** spent in the wilderness, being tempted by the **Devil** (Matthew 4:1–11). ▶See also **Easter**.

Liberation Theology During the 1960s and 1970s, the **Roman Catholic Church** in Latin and South America was surrounded by overwhelming poverty and brutality. Many Catholic **priests** and Church people decided that they must identify themselves totally with the needs of the poor and became involved in political activity. Sometimes this involved joining violent guerilla groups. These followers of Liberation Theology claimed that the teaching of the **Bible** supported their actions. The Roman Catholic Church, however, did not agree and excommunicated some of the priests. ▶See also **excommunication**.

Litany a form of public **prayer** used in Christian **worship**. It involves the leader saying or singing a series of requests (petitions) to God. The people then reply with set responses. A litany is often used when a **priest** and **choir** are in procession.

Liturgy the set form of services of a **Church**. These are usually printed in a service or prayer book which everyone follows. The most important is the **Eucharist** or **Mass**. In the past, some **Protestants** have protested against the use of liturgy

because they have claimed that it limits the freedom of people to worship God as the **Holy Spirit** leads them.

Lord's Day ▶See **Sunday**.

Lord's Prayer the form of words that **Jesus** gave to his **disciples** to teach them how to pray (Matthew 6:9ff). In the **Roman Catholic Church**, it is called the Our Father whilst the **Orthodox Church** refers to it as the Paternoster (Latin for 'Our Father'). There are few services in **church** that do not involve the whole congregation reciting the Lord's Prayer together. See p. 83 for the words of the prayer.

Lord's Supper **Nonconformists** refer to **Holy Communion** as the Lord's Supper or the **Breaking of Bread**. This title is taken directly from the words of **Paul** in 1. Corinthians 11:20. It refers back to the last meal that **Jesus** shared with his **disciples**.

Lourdes the most important Roman Catholic **pilgrimage** destination in southern France. It was there, in 1850, that **Bernadette** Soubirous had several visions of the **Virgin Mary**. Soon a spring of water appeared and several miraculous **healings** were reported. Pilgrims began to make their way to the shrine and now about two million people each year travel to Lourdes in search of **healing**. Bernadette was canonised (made a saint) in 1933.

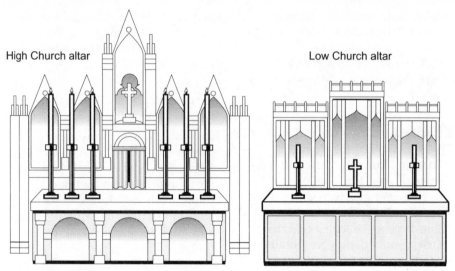

High Church altar

Low Church altar

Unlike High Church, Low Church Anglicans have a simple style of worship with less emphasis on tradition.

Low Church a description often used of some **Anglican churches** which place a very low emphasis on ritual, the value of the **sacraments** and the importance of tradition. Instead, they stress the importance of the **Bible** and a personal experience of God through **Jesus Christ**. Most Low churches are **Evangelical**.

Luke a doctor and the companion of **Paul** on some of his **missionary** journeys. He is regarded as the likely author of the **Gospel** named after him and of the **Acts of the Apostles** – an account of the activities of the first **Christians**. Luke is the patron **Saint** of artists and physicians.

Luther, Martin (1483–1546) a Roman Catholic **monk** who was angered by the sale of **indulgences** to finance the rebuilding of St Peter's Church in Rome. In 1517, he nailed *95 Theses* (beliefs) to his **church** door at Wittenburg and so started the **Protestant Reformation**. After publishing some more writings, Luther was charged with **heresy** and excommunicated from the **Roman Catholic Church** in 1520. ▶ See also **excommunication**.

Lutheran Church a **Protestant** denomination which is based on the teachings of **Martin Luther**. This is the main form of Protestantism in Denmark, Germany, Sweden, Iceland and Norway.

Madonna the **Virgin Mary**. The word is particularly used in connection with statues and pictures of Mary.

Pictures and statues of the Madonna are particularly popular in the Roman Catholic and Orthodox Churches.

Magi the Wise Men who visited the baby **Jesus** shortly after his birth (Matthew 2:1–12). They were the first non-Jews (**Gentiles**) to believe in **Christ**. **Matthew** tells us that they were astrologers, guided from the east by a star and carrying gifts of gold, frankincense and myrrh. They are sometimes known as the Three Kings although their actual number is unknown.

Magisterium the teaching of the **Roman Catholic Church**. It comes from two sources: **1** the **Pope**. Because he has been given the authority of God, he is able to decide on matters of belief on his own when speaking **ex cathedra**. **2** the **bishops** when they meet together in a sacred **Council**. Individual bishops also extend the magisterium when they speak to people in their **diocese** week by week. The teaching **ministry** of the **Church** is going on all the time.

Magnificat taken from the first words of the Latin version of Mary's song praising God, recorded in Luke 1:46–55. Mary sung it after her cousin, Elizabeth, the mother of **John the Baptist**, had greeted her as the mother of God's **Messiah** – **Jesus**. Ever since the 16th century, the song has been widely used in Christian **worship** especially at **Evening Prayer**.

Mark a native of **Jerusalem**, who accompanied **Paul** and Barnabus on their first **missionary** journey. After he left them during the journey, however, Paul refused to take him on his second journey. He is later mentioned as one of the companions of Paul in Rome at the end of his life.

Mark's Gospel the second of the four **Gospels** in the **New Testament**, although it was the first to have been written – in about 65 CE. According to Papias, Mark was largely recording the eye-witness details of **Peter**, one of the **disciples** closest to **Jesus**.

Martyr originally this meant someone who suffers for their beliefs. The early **Christians** were martyrs (witnesses) of **Jesus Christ** (Acts 1:8, 22). Gradually, though, the word came to refer to those who had actually died for their **faith**. There were many Christian martyrs in the 2nd and 3rd centuries and they were highly respected and honoured by the **Church**. Tertullian, who died in 220 CE, wrote: 'The more you cut us down, the more we grow; the seed is the blood of Christians.'

Mass the Roman Catholic name for the **Eucharist**. It comes from the final words in the old Latin service where the people are told '*Ite, missa est*' ('Go, you are dismissed'). As there are many parts of the Mass which are unacceptable to **Protestants**, this service, more than anything else, has divided Protestants and Catholics in the past.

Matins traditionally, it referred to the set time of **prayer** kept by some religious orders at 2 a.m., called the 'night vigil'. In the **Anglican Church**, Matins is the morning service containing **psalms**, **prayers**, two lessons and **collects**. It is also known as Morning Prayer.

Matrimony marriage. **Jesus** underlined the importance of marriage and condemned remarriage (Mark 10:2–12). **Paul** compared the relationship between a husband and wife to that between **Christ** and his **Church** (Ephesians 5:22–33). Within marriage, Paul insisted that husband and wife should have equal rights (1. Corinthians 7:3). The **Book of Common Prayer** states that marriage has three objectives: **a** the procreation (producing) of children. **b** the avoidance of sexual temptation. **c** the mutual support and comfort of the two people.

Matthew described in the **Gospels** as a tax-gatherer, Matthew was one of the twelve **disciples** called to follow **Jesus**. As tax-gatherers were hated by the **Jews** for working for the Romans, this was a controversial choice for Jesus to make. Tradition says that Matthew wrote the first of the Gospels in the **New Testament**. It gives us a picture of Jesus from a very Jewish point of view, as the fulfilment of all the **prophecies** in the **Old Testament**.

Maundy Thursday the day before **Good Friday**, when **Christians** commemorate the first celebration of the **Eucharist** by **Jesus Christ**. The name comes from the Latin word 'mandatum' referring to the 'new commandment' of Jesus to his **disciples** to love one another. On this day every year, the Queen gives **alms** (special coins) to some of her citizens.

Meditation a form of praying used by many **Christians**. It begins by clearing the mind of all distractions by paying attention to such things as breathing, posture, etc. Once freed, the person's mind can then concentrate on God in the hope that he or she will reach a higher state of religious awareness.

Meeting-house the place where **Quakers** come together on **Sunday** mornings to **worship** God. It is quite unlike a **church** since there is no furniture, apart from chairs which are placed round a table where there is usually a **Bible** and some other religious reading material. The Quaker service is one of silence which is only broken if someone feels prompted by the **Holy Spirit** to speak.

Mercy-seat the name given to the platform at which people can kneel in a **Salvation Army citadel**. Traditionally, it is the place to which people come if they want to seek the forgiveness and mercy of God.

Messiah this is the **Hebrew** form of the Greek word **Christ** meaning 'the Anointed One'. The words Messiah and Christ are, therefore, the same. In the **Old Testament**, the **Jews** looked forward to the time when God would send them his Messiah to save them from their enemies. The **Christians**, but not the Jews, believed that **Jesus** was this long-awaited person.

Methodist Church a Christian

denomination, whose members base their **faith** on the teachings of the Anglican clergyman, **John Wesley** (1703–91). The name Methodist was given to the group of serious-minded students, including Wesley, at Oxford University, in the 1720s, who adopted a 'methodical' approach to studying the **Bible** and also lived their lives in an ordered way. Since then, Methodism has spread across the world and is now particularly strong in the USA. Since 1965, the Methodist and **Anglican Churches** have been trying to find a way to unite. So far they have been unsuccessful.

Minister the name given to those who lead the **worship** and preaching

In the Free Church the minister leads worship and preaches and looks after the congregation.

in **Free Churches**. This name underlines their main responsibility – that of ministering to (seeing to the needs of) the people in their congregation. Jesus said, 'Whoever will be great among you, let him be your minister.'

Ministry this is the way that the **church** serves God. Specialised work is performed by those who have been ordained – **priests, deacons, bishops** etc. However, each member has a part to play in the life of the church. It is only when this happens that the church is able to function properly.

Miracle a marvel, an extraordinary event which seems to go against what is known of the laws of nature. To show the love of God, **Jesus** is said to have performed miracles such as the changing of water into wine (John 2), and healing ten men who suffered from leprosy (Luke 17:11–19). **Christians** are divided as to whether miracles, such as **healings**, still take place in the 20th century.

Miserere the 51st **psalm** which begins with the opening words 'Miserere mei, Deus' (Have mercy on me, O Lord). One of the evening services. **Lent** in the **Roman Catholic Church** is called Miserere because this psalm of penitence is read during the worship. A **sermon** or **homily** is then given.

Missal the service book which contains the **prayers, liturgy** and directions for the celebration of the

Mass throughout the year. ▶See also **breviary**.

Missionary someone who is sent out by a **church** to take part in spreading the Christian **Gospel**. Although the early **Christians** were missionaries, the modern missionary movement began at the end of the 18th century, when many people took the message of the Gospel overseas. Now it mainly takes the form of people with special talents in such fields as medicine and education working in countries which have special needs.

Mitre the official head-wear for **bishops** in western countries. It resembles a tall arched and pointed cap. The mitre represents the tongues of fire which fell on the **disciples** on the Day of **Pentecost**. Often decorated with jewels, the colour varies according to the seasons in the **Church Year**.

Monastery the residence of **monks** who live in a community and have taken religious **vows**. The buildings traditionally include a chapel, a refectory or dining room and rooms (cells), where the monks study and sleep. Often the monastery also has outbuildings where the monks do manual work to support the monastery, or fields which are farmed.

Monk a member of a religious order who has accepted, and orders his life by, the three **vows** of poverty, **chastity** and obedience. It is normal for a monk to stay in the same **monastery** for his whole life, although one or two orders encourage them to move around. The modern monk is expected to combine a life of **prayer** and study with some service to the world outside.

Monogamy the practice of men and women only being married to one partner at any one time. This is accepted as the norm throughout the **New Testament**, although important characters in the **Old Testament**, like David and Solomon, had many wives. 'Polygamy' is the practice of being married to more than one partner at the same time.

Monotheism a belief in one God who is personal and separate from the universe. **Christianity, Judaism** and Islam are the three great monotheistic religions. Religions such as Hinduism, which believe in many gods, are polytheistic.

Monsignor a title given in the **Roman Catholic Church** to all **bishops, cardinals** and **archbishops**. It is used together with the **priest's** surname. For example a well-known 19th century Cardinal was called 'Monsignor Newman'.

Morning Prayer ▶See **Matins**.

Moses the leader and law-giver in ancient **Israel**. He led the journey of the Israelites out of Egyptian slavery (called the **Exodus**) and guided them through the wilderness for many years. On Mount Sinai he received the Law from God, including the **Ten Commandments**. He finally died within sight of the Promised Land, Canaan, now called **Israel**.

Mothering Sunday traditionally, the fourth **Sunday** of **Lent**, when people visited their mothers to give them presents. Also, on this day, those people who worshipped in small **chapels** visited the 'mother' church of their **diocese**, or the **cathedral**, to receive some spiritual nourishment. The day comes midway through **Lent** and is also known as Refreshment Sunday, since it provides a temporary break in the Lent fast.

Music musical instruments were not used in **church** until they were introduced in the Middle Ages. The organ began to play an important role in **worship** when **hymns** were written to involve the whole congregation. Today, a wide range of instruments is used with the guitar and drums being particularly popular in services where young people are involved.

Nativity **Christmas** Day which **Christians** set apart to celebrate and remember the birth of **Jesus** in the stable in **Bethlehem**.

Natural family planning a method of birth control that depends on a woman knowing when she is fertile in her monthly menstrual cycle. On those days she abstains from sexual intercourse in order to avoid becoming pregnant. The **encyclical Humanae Vitae** forbade any Roman Catholic to use artificial means of **contraception** such as the Pill, condom, coil etc. Catholics were told that they could only use 'natural family planning'

Nave the main part of a traditional **church** running from the back of the building to the **chancel**. This is the area where the congregation sits. In old churches, it is sometimes separated from the chancel by an ornamental partition called a rood

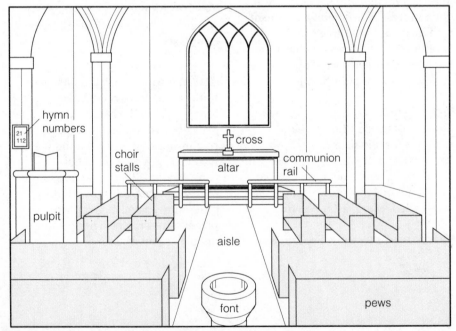

This is the basic plan for most traditional church buildings.

screen. The nave is so-called because it was said to resemble the shape of a ship that is upside down.

Nazareth the village in **Galilee** (north **Israel**) where **Jesus** spent his boyhood and early manhood. He moved to Capernaum to start his public **ministry** because the people in Nazareth had little confidence in him as a teacher (Luke 4:16–30). The early **Christians** were called Nazarenes (Acts 24.5).

New birth many **Christians**, especially **Evangelicals**, believe that a person can only call themselves a Christian if they have undergone a 'conversion experience' – a new birth. There are two sides to this experience: **a** God, through his **Holy Spirit**, acts on a person's 'heart' so that the whole direction of their life changes. **b** a person has to turn to God and seek his pardon and forgiveness.

New English Bible a translation of the **Bible** into modern English produced by the **Protestant Churches** of Britain. The **New Testament** appeared in 1961 and the **Old Testament**, together with the **Apocrypha**, were published five years later. The complete Bible first appeared in 1970.

New Testament the **Bible** is divided into two parts – the **Old Testament** and the New Testament. The New Testament contains those books which were written in the early years of the **Christian Church,** 25 years or more after the **resurrection** of **Jesus**. There are 27 such books in all – four **Gospels**, the **Acts of the Apostles**, the **Epistles** and the Revelation of St **John**.

Nicene Council the first **Church Council**, held in 325 CE. All of the **Church**'s **bishops** were summoned to Nicea by the Roman Emperor, **Constantine**, to deal with the activities of a **heretic** called Arius, who was troubling the Church at the time. The Council tried to set down exactly what **Christians** should believe about **Jesus Christ**.

Nicene Creed the **Nicene Council** produced a **creed**. Additions were made in 381 and this combined statement of Christian belief is called the Nicene Creed. For centuries, it has been widely used in many Christian **Churches**. It is often recited in church services to express the belief of the Church and of individual **Christians**. As with other creeds, the Nicene Creed was used as a way of trying to exclude those people who were thought to be **heretics**. You can find this creed on page 82.

Nonconformists under Queen Elizabeth I, the **Church of England** became the **Established Church** in England. Over the years that followed, however, many people left this Church because they could not accept its teaching. They formed Churches of their own and became known as Nonconformists. Amongst

the Nonconformists are the **Baptists**, the **Congregationalists**, the Presbyterians and the **Quakers**.
▶See also **Presbyterianism**.

Novena a Roman Catholic **prayer** which is extended over a period of nine days for some special purpose or occasion. It is asked for through the **intercession** of the **Virgin Mary** or a **Saint**.

Novice someone who is starting the religious life of a **nun** or a **monk** and has not yet taken their **vows** of poverty, **chastity** and obedience. The period of being a novice lasts for at least a year during which time the person may leave the **monastery** or **convent** – or be asked to do so. At the end of their novitiate, they take their vows.

Nun a woman who is a member of a religious order and has taken vows of poverty, **chastity** and obedience. In the past nuns were set apart from other people by the clothes that they wore – especially the **habit** which was usually black and full length so covering most of the body including the head. Since the **Second Vatican Council**, however, nuns have also

been allowed to wear ordinary clothes. Also fewer nuns have lived in enclosed orders with no contact with the outside world. These barriers have now been broken down and nuns try to combine a life of **prayer** with one of service to the community. Among the most well known orders are the **Poor Clares**, the **Carmelites** and the **Benedictines**.

Nunc dimittis this was Simeon's **prayer** of thanksgiving after he held the baby **Jesus** in his arms when he was presented in the **Temple** in **Jerusalem** (Luke 2:22–35). The title itself comes from Simeon's first two words in Latin which mean 'now lettest thou depart'. The nunc dimittis forms a part of the Anglican service of **Evening Prayer** or Evensong.

Nuptial Mass the **Mass** or **Eucharist** service which is part of the wedding service in a **Roman Catholic Church**. Since 1966 it has been permitted in **marriages** where only one of the people is a Roman Catholic. The non-Catholic, however, may not receive **Holy Communion** during the service.

Oblate a person who is not ordained nor has taken religious **vows** but is attached to a **monastery** or doing religious work. Such people have often given their possessions to the monastery. The name comes from the Latin, meaning 'offered up'.

Offertory during the **Mass**, members of the congregation bring forward their offerings of **bread** and wine to be 'offered up' to God. At the same time the **choir** 'offer up' an **anthem** as part of the people's **worship**.

Oil olive oil is consecrated (set aside for holy use) by Roman Catholic

Consecrated oil is used to anoint people when they are sick.

bishops each **Maundy Thursday** for **churches** in their **dioceses** in the coming year. In some churches it is used when **prayers** for the sick and dying are offered and the person is anointed (smeared with oil). It is also used in the ceremonies of **baptism, confirmation** and **ordination**. In the **New Testament**, oil was believed to have **healing** properties (James 5:14) and it is still a symbol of this today. ►See also **anointing**.

Old Testament the Christian title for the books of the Jewish **Scriptures**, which are divided into three sections – the Law (**Torah**), the Prophets and the Writings. The same books are found in the Christian **Bible** but they are in a different order. For the first few decades of the **Church**'s existence the Jewish Scriptures were all that the Church possessed. ►See also **New Testament**.

Ordination the service through which a man or a woman is admitted to holy orders and so becomes a **priest**. Before a person can be ordained, they must be baptised and confirmed. In the **Roman Catholic, Anglican** and **Orthodox Churches** there are three different orders of **ministry** –

deacons, priests and **bishops** – and each one of them is conferred on a person by a bishop through ordination. Of these three **Churches**, the Anglican Church is the only one as yet to ordain women. This it has done since 1994, a move which has caused a lot of heated argument with some people leaving the Anglican Church.

Ordination of women
after a long, and painstaking debate in the **Church of England**, the decision to ordain women to the priesthood was put into practice in 1994. Many people disagreed with the move and even as women were being ordained some of those totally opposed to it were leaving the **Church** and becoming Roman Catholics. More recent debate has centred around the question of whether women can become **bishops** as they have done in many parts of the **Anglican Communion**.

Original sin
the **sin** by the first man and woman in the Garden of Eden. Most **Churches**, though not all **Christians**, believe that because of this, every member of the human race is a sinner from the moment they are born. Some Christians hold that original sin is forgiven at **baptism** and that its effects are taken away by living a holy life. Roman Catholics believe that the **Virgin Mary**, the mother of **Jesus**, is the only human being, apart from her

son, to be born without original sin.
▶ See also **Immaculate Conception**.

Orthodox Church
a family of different **Churches** which are mainly found in eastern Europe and the Middle East. They broke away from the **Roman Catholic Church** in the **Great Schism** of 1054. The form of **worship** of these Churches is very elaborate and there is extensive use of **icons**. The different Orthodox Churches have their own patriarchs.

Priests in the Orthodox Church have more elaborate vestments than in the Western Church.

Our Father
▶ See **Lord's Prayer**.

Pacifism an approach to life which means a person is against all forms of violence, including fighting in a war. Love and not violence is the basic principle of this way of life. Although a person does not have to be a **Christian** to be a pacifist, there are many Christian pacifists, although only one **denomination** – the **Quakers** – is openly committed to it. Christian pacifists point out that **Jesus** said that peacemaking was a mark of all genuine Christians (Matthew 5:9). ▶See also **conscientious objection**.

Padre in Latin America and many other countries this is the form of address for a **priest**. It is also a popular name for a priest in the armed forces.

Palestine when the **Jews** left Egypt and their life of slavery behind them, God promised them a home of their own called the Promised Land. This was Canaan which later came to be called Palestine (see map above). It was home to the Jews until the Romans captured **Jerusalem** in 70 CE. The Jews were then scattered and the land was only returned to them in 1948 when the State of **Israel** was formed.

Palm Sunday the last **Sunday** of **Lent** and the beginning of **Holy**

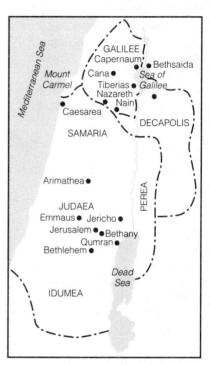

At various times, this land has been called Canaan, Palestine and Israel. It was also referred to as the Promised Land.

Week. It was on this day that **Jesus** rode into **Jerusalem** on a donkey and the people spread palm leaves on the road in front of him (Matthew 21:1–9). Small palm **crosses** are often given out during **church** services as a reminder of this. In some parish churches there is a procession when members of the congregation walk behind a donkey waving palm crosses. Palm branches have often been used in the Church's history to symbolise triumph, glory and victory over **sin**.

Papacy the system of government in the **Roman Catholic Church** headed by the **Pope**. Some Roman Catholics believe that the papacy has authority over all the **Christian Churches** but most **Protestants** would not agree with this. To Roman Catholics, the Pope is the Vicar of Christ (his representative) on earth and the guardian of the **faith**.

Pantocrator this means the Lord of all. In Orthodox **churches**, there is often a large painting stretched right across the inside of the dome of **Christ** the Pantocrator. He is seated on a throne and in one hand he holds the roll of the law whilst the other is raised in a gesture of command.

Parables short stories, or sayings, based upon everyday experiences. **Jesus** used them mainly to show his followers how they should behave or to illustrate God's kingdom on earth. Almost 80 parables of Jesus are recorded in the **Gospels**. Some of them, such as the parable of the mustard seed, can be found in all four Gospels.

Paraclete literally the advocate or legal helper in a court of law. The name was used by **Jesus** to refer to the **Holy Spirit** who would be sent by God to his **disciples** as a comforter and helper and to guide

them in their work in the world (see John 14–16).

Parish a geographical area under the spiritual care of a **Church of England vicar** or a Roman Catholic **priest**.

Paschal candle the word 'paschal' comes from the **Hebrew** for Passover and relates to the festival of **Easter** (the Christian Passover). The Paschal **candle**, which is lit in many **churches** on **Holy Saturday**, symbolises the light of the risen **Christ**. It stays alight for the 40 days between Easter and **Ascension Day**.

Passion the physical and mental sufferings of **Jesus Christ** which led up to his death on the **cross**.

Passion play these were common in Europe from the 14th century onwards and concentrated on the story of the **passion** of **Jesus**. The best known example is the Oberammergau Passion Play which takes place every ten years. In 1633, a great number of people in the village were killed by the Black Death and the survivors vowed to perform a passion play there once a decade ever since. The cast of the play is still drawn from the villagers.

Passion Sunday the **Sunday** before **Palm Sunday** when the sufferings of **Jesus** on the **cross**, both physical and spiritual, are remembered.

Passover the most important festival in the Jewish calendar. In

Hebrew it is called Pesach. It commemorates the **exodus** of the **Jews** from slavery in Egypt, and is celebrated mainly in the home with a symbolic meal and the Seder service. Today the festival is also a reminder of other times when the Jewish people have suffered greatly – particularly during the **Holocaust** in the Second World War.

Pastor the name, meaning 'shepherd', which **Free Churches** often give to the **minister** of a **church**.

Paten a small plate used to cover the **chalice** and on which the wafers of **bread** are placed during the **Eucharist**.

Pater noster the first two words of the Latin version of the 'Our Father', the **Lord's Prayer**. Every eleventh bead on a **rosary** is called the paternoster because the Lord's Prayer is repeated when the bead is reached.

Patriarch this title was used in the 6th century for the five most important **bishops** of the ancient **Church** – Rome, Antioch, Alexandria, Constantinople and **Jerusalem**. More recently the title has been used by the **Orthodox Churches** of their senior bishops of Constantinople, Alexandria and **Jerusalem**.

Paul of Tarsus Saul of Tarsus was a **Pharisee** who saw it as his duty to wipe out the newly formed **Christian Church**. Whilst doing this

he had a vision of **Christ** on the Damascus Road and was converted (Acts 9:1–9). After this he changed his name to Paul and became **Christianity**'s first **missionary**. He founded many **churches** across the Roman Empire. He shaped the beliefs of the early **Christians** by writing many letters – some of which are found in the **New Testament**. He was probably martyred in Rome around 65 CE.

Pax the 'kiss of peace,' sometimes a handshake which is given at **Mass**. The only time when this does not happen is **Maundy Thursday**.

Penance one of the seven **sacraments** of the **Roman Catholic Church**. In it, a person seeks forgiveness of God for their **sins** by confessing (admitting) them to a **priest**. There are four parts to the sacrament: **a** contrition – being sorry for your sins. **b** a **confession** of the sins to the priest. This sacrament is also sometimes called confession. **c** absolution – the forgiveness of God given through the priest. **d** satisfaction – doing the penance or punishment set by the priest. In the Roman Catholic Church penance has been called the Rite of Reconciliation since the **Second Vatican Council**.

Pentecost the Greek name for the Jewish Feast of Weeks, when the first fruits of the harvest were presented to God. It took place 50 days after **Passover**. As the first **disciples** were celebrating Pentecost, ten days after the **ascension** of **Jesus**, the **Holy Spirit** came down on them (Acts 2). The Day of Pentecost is often called the birthday of the **Christian Church**. It is also known as Whitsun.

Pentecostal Movement

a movement amongst **Protestant Christians** which began in 1901 in the USA although it is now world-wide. To Pentecostal Christians the **baptism** in the **Holy Spirit**, similar to that experienced by the **disciples** on the Day of **Pentecost**, is very important. Pentecostal services are very enthusiastic, with much **speaking in tongues** and **healing** taking place.

Perpetual virginity of Mary

the Roman Catholic belief that Mary did not have sexual intercourse either before or after the birth of **Jesus**. The brothers of Jesus mentioned in Matthew 12:46 are not thought to be actual sons of Mary but of her husband Joseph from a previous marriage.

Peter

a fisherman and the brother of **Andrew**. One of the original **disciples** of **Jesus**. His name was Simon but he was soon called Peter (the rock). He was the natural leader of the disciples and was given the special job of looking after the **Church** by Jesus after his **resurrection** (John 21:15–19). According to tradition, he was made the first **Bishop** of **Rome (Pope)** where he was martyred around the same time as **Paul** – probably 65 CE. Roman Catholics believe that his authority has been handed down to

all who have held the office of Pope after him. ▶ See also **apostolic succession**.

Pew

the fixed wooden seating in a **Church**. Originally the body of a church was an empty space with benches around the walls for those unable to stand. Pews were then gradually added with special pews set aside for the most important church members.

Pharisees

an important Jewish religious group at the time of **Jesus**. Their aim was not only to obey the written law of **Moses** (the **Torah**) but also the unwritten interpretations of that law – called the 'traditions of the elders'. They separated themselves from everything they thought impure – hence their name meaning 'the Separated Ones'. Jesus came into conflict with them because their approach to religion was very different from his own.

Pilgrimage

a holy journey which is made to a **shrine** or a **sanctuary** which is thought to be holy. Pilgrims make the journey for a variety of reasons – a sense of duty; thankfulness to God or to a **saint**; to ask for **healing**; to give thanks for **blessings** that have been received, as a **penance**, or simply out of curiosity. In the Christian religion members do not have to make such journeys – they are undertaken voluntarily. Most of them are made by Roman Catholics. Amongst the most popular shrines visited are **Lourdes** in France, Santiago de

Compostela in Spain and **Walsingham** in Norfolk.

Pontiff this means 'high priest'. In the **Roman Catholic Church** it refers to the **Pope** although it was originally applied to any **bishop**. The length of time for which a Pope reigns is called the pontificate.

Pontius Pilate the Roman governor, or procurator, of Judea from 26 CE to 36 CE. After **Jesus** had appeared before the **High Priest**, he was brought in front of Pilate since he alone could give the order for Jesus to be put to death. He later fell out with his Roman masters, was dismissed and, if tradition is to be believed, committed suicide.

Poor Clares a religious order for women founded by **St Francis of Assisi** and Clare, a **nun** who made her **vows** of poverty, **chastity** and obedience in front of Francis. Shortly after its founding in 1213, members of the order turned to a life of total poverty. It became the most highly disciplined of all the Roman Catholic religious orders.

Pope the title given to the **Bishop** of Rome, the successor of St **Peter** and the leader of the **Roman Catholic Church** thoughout the world. The Pope, or the Holy Father or Papa as he is sometimes called, has the authority to teach all Catholics on matters of Christian **faith** and behaviour and to guide the affairs of the Roman Catholic Church on earth There have been 263 Popes altogether of which 209 have been from Italy.

Prayer the approach of human beings to God. In the Christian tradition it can include many different elements: **a** praise – for God alone deserves to be worshipped. **b confession** of **sin** – because before God, human beings are very aware of their own sinfulness. **c** petition and **intercession** – asking that one's own needs (petition) and those of others (intercession) might be met. **d** thanksgiving – being thankful to God for past **blessings** and help. In Roman Catholicism prayers are also directed to the **Virgin Mary** and the **Saints.**

Presbyter an **elder** in the early **Church**, responsible for guiding believers, baptising converts, preaching and teaching, and leading the congregation in **prayer** and praise to God. ▶ See also **Presbyterianism**.

Presbyterianism a system of **church** government directed by **elders** (**presbyters**) and adopted by some members of the Church, mainly in Scotland, who took the name Presbyterian. It was based on the ideas of the great **Protestant** reformer John Calvin (1509–64) who, with **Martin Luther**, led the Protestant **Reformation** in Europe.

Priest the title given to people who are authorised to lead **worship** in the **Anglican**, **Roman Catholic** and

Orthodox Churches. Of these three Churches, the Anglican Church is the only one to ordain women as priests. Priests are given their authority when they are ordained by a **bishop**. This means that they alone can administer the **sacraments**. Most people consider this to be the main responsibility of a priest. ▶ See also **ordination**.

The main duty of a priest is to administer the sacraments.

Primate the title which is given to the **bishop** who occupies the first or main position of authority in the **Church**. In the case of the **Church of England**, this is the **Archbishop of Canterbury** who is called the Primate of All England. The Archbishop of York, the next most important office, is called the Primate of England.

Prior, Prioress, Priory a prior is the head or the assistant to the **abbot** in a monastic community of men. A prioress is either the head or the assistant to the **abbess** in a monastic community of women. A priory is a small monastic community which is attached to an **abbey**. ▶ See also **monastery, monk**.

Prophecy 1 God's verdict on a present situation. 2 God's word about what is going to happen in the future. The prophets in the **Old Testament** were looked on as inspired teachers with a message from God. They spoke to the people about the past, the present and the future. They were mainly concerned, however, with the present. They tried to give the people a clear idea about the character of God and the duty which individuals had to him. In the **New Testament**, prophecy was, according to **Paul**, one of the gifts which the **Holy Spirit** had made to the **Church**. (Romans 12:6).

Prostration the act of bowing oneself to the ground as a sign of humility and respect. When **cardinals** receive the symbols of their office (position), they prostrate themselves before the **Pope**.

Protestant a **Christian** who does not belong to either the **Orthodox** or the **Roman Catholic Churches**. Originally Protestants were so-called because they 'protested' against certain practices of the Catholic

Church. There are many Protestant **denominations** but all are united in their belief that the **Bible** is the supreme authority for all Christians.

Psalm a song which is intended to be chanted or sung during religious services or ceremonies. The Book of Psalms in the **Old Testament** is a collection of these songs – most of which were written to be sung in the **Temple** in **Jerusalem**. Psalms have been used as a part of Christian **worship** for centuries, although they have become less popular in recent years. Of the 150 psalms in the Old Testament, 73 are said to have been written by King David.

Pulpit an elevated platform at the front of a **church** from which the **priest** delivers a **sermon** during a service. In modern **Protestant** churches, the pulpit is often in the centre of the church. Its high position emphasises that the preaching of God's Word is above everything else.

Purgatory According to Roman Catholic belief, purgatory is the place in which the **soul** is purified after death. Only after time spent in purgatory is the soul ready to enter into God's presence and enjoy the **beatific vision**.

Pyx a small metal receptacle or box, used mainly by Roman Catholic **priests** to take the **reserved sacrament** to people in their homes if they are unable to go to **church**. The pyx is also used in churches to store the **host**.

Q the symbol for the non-existent document which was thought to have been used by **Matthew** or **Luke**, or both, when writing their **Gospels**. In the **Synoptic Gospels** there is much material common to both Matthew and Luke – and thought to come from this document. The passages concerned consist mainly of the sayings of **Jesus**.

Quakers a Christian **denomination** which started in the 17th century through the activities of George Fox. In their meetings Quakers wait for the **Holy Spirit** to speak in and through them and this 'voice' is called the Inner Light. The Quakers do not have any **ministers** or **priests**, nor do they celebrate any of the **sacraments**. Quakers do not believe in war or the use of force – they are pacifists. ▶See also **conscientious objection, pacifism**.

R

Racism any form of behaviour or speech based on the assumption that one group of people is inferior to another. Racism is usually, but not always, based on the colour of the person, or group, being discriminated against.

Reader in the **Church of England** a person who is not ordained but is licensed by a **bishop** to conduct certain services. He or she can take **Morning** or **Evening Prayer** but cannot give **absolution** or pronounce a **blessing**. They cannot conduct the **Eucharist**.

Real presence the belief held by Roman Catholics that **Christ** is actually present in the **bread** and wine in the **Mass** after it has been consecrated.

Reconciliation the restoration of the human race to a state of friendship with God. In Christian belief, human beings became the enemies of God after the **sin** of the first man and woman. **Paul** often spoke of reconciliation which he put down to the death and **resurrection** of **Jesus** (Romans 5:10; Ephesians 2:13). ▶ See also **original sin, redemption**.

Rector in the past, a person who received the tithes (gifts of money or produce) from people in the village. Now the word means just the same as a **vicar**.

Redemption the act of rescuing or freeing. The **Old Testament** presents God as the Redeemer of **Israel** who delivered (freed) his people from slavery in Egypt. The New Testament shows **Jesus** as liberating (redeeming) people through his death and **resurrection** (Romans 3:24; Ephesians 1:7).

Reformation the religious revolution which took place in the western **Church** in the 16th century. It was begun by **Martin Luther** in 1517 at Wittenburg when he pinned up *95 Theses* (beliefs) to his church door. He and his followers did not agree with such Church practices as the selling of **indulgences**. When the Church excommunicated Luther for **heresy**, **Protestant** churches began to be formed.

Relic the remains of **saints** or holy people or some article or item of clothing connected with them. Because of their close association with such a holy person, relics are treated with great reverence by members of the **Roman Catholic** and **Orthodox Church**. This practice is rejected by **Protestants** as superstition.

Repentance the act of repenting or turning one's back on **sins** that have been committed. Repentance is an important Christian idea, showing a change of mind that leads to a change of direction in a person's life. In the case of a **Christian**, this means turning from a self-centred life to one that is centred on God.

Requiem a **Mass** in the **Roman Catholic Church** which is said for those who have died. The name comes from the time when the service was said in Latin and began with the words '*Requiem aeternam donam eis, Domine*' (Give them eternal rest, O Lord).

Reserved Sacrament the practice, followed in Roman Catholic, Orthodox and some Anglican **churches**, of keeping consecrated **bread** (rarely wine) from a **Mass** or **Eucharist** to use later. It is stored in a **pyx**. **Holy Communion** can then be given to sick people in their own homes.

Resurrection one of the beliefs found in the **Apostles Creed** that all believers will rise from the dead on the last day after **Christ** returns to the earth. This is based firmly on the belief that Christ returned to life after being dead for three days.
▶ See also **Second Coming**.

Resurrection of Christ the rising of **Jesus** from the dead three days after he was crucified which is the central belief of **Christianity**. **Paul** described this as 'the first fruits of them that slept' (1. Corinthians 15:20–1). He was saying that the resurrection of Jesus guaranteed the resurrection of all Christian believers from the dead to share in the kingdom of **heaven**. **Christians** celebrate this at **Easter**.

Retreat a period of withdrawal from the world for quiet spiritual reflection and thought. A retreat is usually held in a **monastery** or a **convent** under the direction of an experienced leader.

Revelation this refers to God revealing himself (making himself known) to humankind. **Christians** believe that the human race could know nothing of God if he had not chosen to reveal himself. This happens in two ways: **a** through the universe, the world of nature and the human conscience. **b** through the events in the **Bible** – and particularly through **Jesus Christ**.

Ritual a form of words set out in a service or prayer book for a particular occasion. Apart from the **Eucharist**, most of the rituals in the **Christian Church** are to mark important human experiences. These are called rites of passage and include **baptism**, shortly after birth, **confirmation** at the outset of puberty, marriage (**matrimony**) to start a family, and burial at the end of life.

Rogation Days the three days before **Ascension Day**. Traditionally these days have been days of **prayer** and **fasting** offered up to God for a good harvest. On Rogation Sunday (the **Sunday** before Ascension), processions used to take place to say prayers in the local fields. This tradition is still continued in a few country areas.

Roman Catholic Church the community of **Christians** throughout the world which follows the leadership of the **Pope**, as the successor of St **Peter** on earth. It is the largest of all the Christian **denominations** with 1,000 million followers world-wide. ▶See also **apostolic succession, Pope, Rome**.

Rome founded, according to legend, by Romulus in 763 BCE and named after him. Known as 'the Eternal City', Rome became the home of the **papacy** in 756. **Paul** died in Rome and **Peter** was its first **Bishop** (**Pope**). Most of the papal ceremonies take place in the **Basilica** of St Peter in Rome, the largest **church** in the world.

Rosary a series of **prayers** which is particularly popular amongst older Roman Catholics. The name is also used for the string of beads which pass through the hands of the person saying the prayers. The beads are divided up into five groups with a large bead in between. Working their way through all the beads enables a worshipper to meditate on various episodes (mysteries) in the life of **Jesus** and his mother, Mary. Each **meditation** is followed by the **Hail Mary** (**Ave Maria**) said several times, the **Lord's Prayer** and the Gloria Patri.

The rosary is used by Roman Catholics to guide them as they pray.

S

Sabbath Day the seventh day of the Jewish week and set apart by God's command for **worship**, rest and recreation (Deuteronomy 5:14). **Christians** began by observing the Sabbath Day, which is Saturday, but they soon set aside **Sunday**, the first day of the week, for worship. This was because **Jesus** rose from the dead on this day.

Sacrament an outward, physical sign of an inward, spiritual **blessing**. Protestants believe that there are just two sacraments – **baptism** and the **Eucharist** or **Lord's Supper** – since these are the only ones that can be traced back directly to the **ministry** of **Jesus**. Roman Catholics and Orthodox believers, however, celebrate seven sacraments – although the **Orthodox Church** prefers to call them mysteries. These are **baptism**, **Holy Communion**, **confirmation**, **matrimony** (marriage), **ordination**, **penance** (**confession**) and **extreme unction**.

Sadducees the priests of the **Temple** in **Jerusalem** at the time of **Jesus**. They were disliked by the **Jews** because they co-operated with the Romans who occupied the city. Although they co-operated with the **Pharisees** who were against Jesus, the two groups did not get on well with each other. Nothing more is heard of them after the destruction of the city of **Jerusalem** by the Romans in 70 CE

Saint a person who is exceptionally holy and leads a life of devotion to God. In the **New Testament**, all **Christians** are called to be saints serving a holy God. Soon, however, the word was applied only to those who had lived outstanding lives – and who had often been martyred. The **Roman Catholic Church** sometimes recognises a person's exceptional personal devotion by canonising them. However, this is rare today. In Christian art, saints are usually shown with a **halo** round their heads. ▶ See also **canonisation**.

Salvation being saved from **sin**. **Christians** believe that through the death and **resurrection** of **Jesus**, God saves human beings from the power of sin. God also gives them the free gift of eternal life and membership of his kingdom on earth. ▶ See also **Kingdom of God**.

Salvation Army an international **Protestant** organisation started by William Booth in 1878, which is organised along military lines with its own special uniform. When it began, the Army went out into the streets of London to wage a war against every evil – poverty, alcohol and so on – and it still does similar work today. Its members are called soldiers and it has officers who lead but no **priests**. They do not celebrate any **sacraments** and a brass band plays an important part in their **worship**.

The Salvation Army flag – a symbol of hope for the poor and needy.

Sanctification the process of either being or being made holy and pure. In the **Bible**, God alone is holy and pure by nature. God's people are made pure because they believe in him. For Catholics, such holiness largely comes through the **sacraments** whilst **Protestants** stress the need for **faith**.

Sanctuary the area in a **church** where the **altar** is located. If there is more than one altar, it is the area around the high (main) altar. In Orthodox churches, the sanctuary is enclosed by the **iconostasis**.

Sanhedrin at the time of **Jesus**, this was the highest Jewish court, with 71 members. It met in **Jerusalem** and was given authority over the whole of Judea. It is not clear whether the Sanhedrin had the power to pass the death penalty or not so we do not know whether it played any part in the death of Jesus.

Satan in the **Bible**, he is a supernatural being who is the main enemy of God, the leader of all the rebellious **angels** and the source of all evil in the world. Also known as the Devil, Satan tried to tempt **Jesus** at the start of his **ministry** (Matthew 4:1–11). **Christians** believe that although he will finally be defeated at the end of time, at the moment Satan is free to carry on his evil work in the world (2. Corinthians 2:11).

Schism a division between two groups of people. In the **Church**, a schism takes place when a group of people break away from the main Church. The most important schism in the Church's history took place in 1054 when the **Orthodox Church** was formed after breaking away from the **Roman Catholic Church** (the **Great Schism**). In the 18th century, another schism took place when the **Methodist Church** broke away from the **Church of England**.

Scribe in the **New Testament**, a Jewish interpreter and teacher of the law of Moses. Usually linked with the **Pharisees** in their opposition to **Jesus**. Two incidents involving scribes are recorded in Matthew 22.35 and Mark 12.28.

Scriptures the collection of books inspired by God and known as the **Bible**.

Second Coming the time when **Christ** will return to the earth to set up his kingdom. Most **Christians** believe in, and look forward to, this. It will, however, be quite unlike his 'first coming', which was as a baby in **Bethlehem**. This time he will return in glory and in power (Matthew 24:29ff). ▶ See also **Kingdom of God**.

Second Vatican Council also known as the 21st Ecumenical **Council** of the **Roman Catholic Church**, this met between 1962 and 1965. It was called by Pope John XXIII (1958–63) who expressed his wish to open the windows of the **Church** to let in some fresh air. The Council had a great effect on the **worship** and life of the Catholic Church ending, for example, the tradition that all services should be conducted in Latin. It also encouraged much greater involvement of the **laity**.

See the seat or throne of a **bishop**. The town or city in which a **cathedral** is situated.

Septuagint the Greek version of the **Hebrew Bible**. Tradition has it that 72 scholars were commissioned to translate the **Scriptures** in the 3rd century BCE, which they did in 72 days agreeing on every word – even though they worked independently of one another!

Sermon the part of the service where the **priest** or **minister** explains some aspect of Christian belief or a passage from the **Bible**. In the **Roman Catholic Church** it is known as the **homily**. The sermon is considered to be particularly important in **Nonconformist** churches where there is a strong belief that it is the preaching of the **Gospel** which can bring men and women to **salvation**. ▶ See also **homily**.

Sermon on the mount the title given to the teachings of **Jesus** in Matthew 5–7. It is unlikely, though, that it was ever a **sermon** delivered on a mountain! It is probably a collection of Jesus' sayings brought together by **Matthew** himself. It includes both the **Beatitudes** and the **Lord's Prayer**.

Shema the Jewish name for the words recorded in Deuteronomy 6:4: 'Hear, O Israel, the Lord our God, the Lord is One.' This statement of belief stands at the very heart of the Jewish **faith** and it is still recited in Jewish homes and in the **synagogue**.

Shrine originally a structure containing the bones of a **saint**. It is now applied to any place which has strong religious connections. Such shrines as St Peter's in Rome and the Church of the Holy Sepulchre in **Jerusalem** have become centres of **pilgrimage**.

Shrove Tuesday the day before **Ash Wednesday** when the fast of **Lent** begins. The name is taken from an old word 'to shrive' which meant 'to hear a **confession** and grant **absolution**'. This was the day when people confessed their **sins** of the past year and asked for God's forgiveness through the **priest**.

Sign of the cross the tracing of the shape of the **cross** over one's own body or that of someone else. In western **Churches**, the movement of the hand is from the head to breast to left shoulder. In the **Orthodox** Church, it is from right to left across the shoulders. **Christians** often cross themselves in church when they stand in front of the **altar**, or when they are about to undertake a particularly demanding task.

Sin an action which is against the known will of God. It is a word frequently used by **Christians**. Roman Catholics draw a distinction between very serious sins which cause spiritual death (mortal) and those which are less serious (venial). Sins can be a deliberate act by someone (sin of commission) or a failure to carry out a command of God (sin of omission).

Son of God a title given in the **Bible** to the **Messiah**. Applied to **Jesus**, it underlines his relationship with God.

Soul the soul or spirit are words which **Christians** use when talking of someone's innermost being. It is through this spiritual side of a person that God is worshipped.

Speaking in tongues the practice in the early **Church**, and in a few modern **denominations**, of praying and speaking in an unknown language in the **church** during **worship**. It occurs when a person is carried away with emotion. ▶See also **glossolalia**.

Stations of the cross these are the fourteen carvings or paintings around the walls of Roman Catholic **churches**, which trace the path of **Christ** from the time he was condemned by **Pontius Pilate** to the time when he was nailed to the **cross**. This is sometimes called the Way of the Cross. In many modern churches a fifteenth, showing the **resurrection**, is also added. As part of the **worship** on **Good Friday**, members of the congregation make their way from picture to picture praying and meditating on the event shown. ▶See also **meditation**.

Stephen the first Christian **martyr** who was stoned to death in the presence of Saul who was later **Paul**. He was killed for preaching to the **Jews** that **Jesus** was the long promised **Messiah**. The death probably took place in 36 CE.

Stoup a vessel or bowl, in Roman Catholic and some Anglican **churches**, which holds **holy water**. Worshippers dip their fingers into the stoup as they enter church and cross themselves.

Suffragan bishop a **bishop** who does not have a **see** of his own but is appointed to help another bishop.

Two of the fourteen scenes, or stations of the cross, showing Christ on the way to his death on the cross.

Sunday meaning the 'day of the sun', this is the first day of the week, the Lord's Day, on which the early **Christians** met to 'break **bread**' (Acts 20:7) and make a collection for the poor. As this was the day on which **Jesus** rose from the dead, it was the natural time to set aside for Christian **worship**.

Sunday school classes for children to teach them about religion. First set up in Gloucester in 1780 by Robert Raikes to teach children to read so that they could read the **Bible**.

Surplice the white linen **vestment** worn by **clergy** and choristers over their **cassocks**.

Symbol something which stands for, and expresses the meaning of, something which is closely associated with it. It is different from a sign which represents something that is different from it – for example, a green light is a sign that means 'go'. At one level, the **sacraments** are signs of God's **blessing**, but at a deeper level they are symbols usually of events which have taken place in **Jesus'** life. The same goes for the central Christian symbols of the **cross** and the **crucifix**.

Synagogue the building in which a Jewish congregation meets for **worship**. The word itself means 'coming together'. Both **Jesus** (Luke 4:16) and **Paul** (Acts 17:1, 2) preached in synagogues. Later on, **Christians** were expelled from synagogues and began to meet in each other's houses.

Synoptic Gospels this is the name given to the first three Gospels – **Matthew, Mark** and **Luke**. The word itself means 'seeing together' indicating that these Gospels have a very similar outlook on the life of **Jesus**, sharing, as they do, much of their material. The most likely explanation for this is that both Matthew and Luke used Mark's Gospel as well as another source, **Q**, in addition to material which is only found in their own Gospels, called M and L.

Taize Community a community of **Protestant monks** founded in Burgundy, in France, in 1944. It began when its **prior**, Roger Schulze, gave refuge in his home to **Jews** and other refugees in war-striken France. Its members, who take **vows** of poverty, **chastity** and obedience, come from many different Christian traditions including Roman Catholic. Visitors are able to spend a short time living with the community.

Te Deum a well-known **hymn** in the Anglican and **Roman Catholic Churches**, so called from the opening words 'Te Deum laudamus' (Thee, God, we praise'). It is thought to have been written in Latin in the 4th century and is included in **Matins**.

Temple a centre of **pilgrimage** in **Jerusalem** for all **Jews**, especially during the great festivals. However, **Jesus** criticised the Temple authorities for turning it into a place of business rather than **worship**. The first Temple in Jerusalem was built by Solomon in 950 BCE. It was destroyed by the Babylonians in 586 BCE. A second Temple was dedicated in 516 BCE but was never completed. **Herod the Great** began rebuilding it in 19 BCE but this, the last Temple, was destroyed by the Romans in 70 CE.

Ten Commandments laws which were given by God to **Moses** on Mount Sinai (Exodus 20:1–17). **Jesus** accepted that they set out the moral demands that God made on everyone (Matthew 5:17). They are occasionally used in **church** services as a summary of the duties that people have towards God.

Thirty-nine Articles a statement of the beliefs held by the **Church of England**, dating from the 16th century. Although these articles are not used in **worship**, they are printed in the **Book of Common Prayer**. Each person who is to be ordained a **deacon** or **priest** is asked to show that they accept the Articles.

Three hours service held in many **churches** on **Good Friday** between noon and 3 a.m. These are thought to have been the hours leading up to the death of **Jesus** on the **cross**.

Torah this can be used generally to mean any teaching but in particular to refer to God's law which is found in the first five books of the **Old Testament**. Together these books are often called the Torah.

Tradition the teaching and practice of the **Church** over the centuries. It is handed down from generation to generation along with the **Bible**. Since the **Reformation**,

Protestants have rejected the idea that tradition is binding on **Christians**. In the **Roman Catholic** and **Orthodox Churches**, however, it still plays a very important role.

Transfiguration the miraculous change in the appearance of Christ when he was on a mountain with three of his **disciples** – **Peter**, James and **John** (Matthew 17:1–9). The event is commemorated by some **churches** on August 6th.

Transubstantiation the official teaching of the **Roman Catholic Church** that in the **Mass**, the **bread** and wine turn, after the prayer of **consecration**, into the actual body and blood of **Christ**. This means that Christ is actually present at the altar. This **doctrine** was first put forward in 1215 and confirmed at the **Council of Trent** in 1551.

Trinity the central **doctrine** (teaching) of the Christian **faith** that there are three persons in One God – God the **Father**, God the Son and God the **Holy Spirit**. **Christianity** does not teach that there are three Gods. God is One and God is Three – One in Three and Three in One: **a** God the Father created the world and sent his Son to save it. **b** God the Son was born as a human being, lived on earth, died and rose again before returning to his Father in **heaven**. **c** Jesus promised that once he left the earth the Holy Spirit would come and enter into people's hearts and minds.

U

United Reformed Church the **Church** which resulted from the joining together of the Congregational and Presbyterian Churches. This took place in 1972 and created a **denomination** with some 130,000 members. The combined Church emphasises the central importance of the **Bible**, making extensive use of it in its **worship**. ▶ See also **Congregationalists, Presbyterianism**.

V

Vatican the residence of the **Pope** and a small, independent city-state in the middle of Rome. Vatican City is the administrative centre of the **Roman Catholic Church**.

Veneration of the cross a Roman Catholic ceremony performed on **Good Friday**. A **crucifix** is placed at the entrance to the **sanctuary** and the people kneel in front of it and kiss it. The **Orthodox Church** carries out a similar ceremony on Holy Cross Day (September 14th).

Vestments special garments which are worn by the **clergy** when they take part in services of **worship**. These include the **cassock**, stole and **chasuble**.

Via Dolorosa means literally 'mournful way'. It refers to the journey taken by **Christ** from the judgement hall of **Pontius Pilate** to his death on Calvary. The same route is followed today by thousands of pilgrims, some of them carrying crosses, when they visit **Jerusalem**.

Viaticum the **Eucharist** or **Holy Communion** which is given to a person who is dying. It is assumed that it will be the last time that they take it and it is therefore intended to provide them with 'spiritual food' for the journey ahead beyond death.

Vicar in the **Church of England**, a vicar is someone who is in charge of a **parish**. In some parishes the vicar is called a **rector**.

Virgin birth the Christian teaching that Mary conceived **Jesus** through the **Holy Spirit** without having had sexual intercourse (Matthew 1; Luke 1, 2). Roman Catholics, in particular, have laid stress on this belief. Its importance is that it makes Jesus free from **original sin**.

Virgin Mary the mother of **Jesus**. By the 16th century, Roman Catholics were saying **prayers** to Mary, showing great reverence towards her and placing statues of her in their **churches**. In 1950, Pope Pius III declared the **doctrine** of the **Assumption of the Virgin Mary** and in 1964, Pope Paul VI declared her to be the Mother of the Church.

Virginity a man or a woman who has never had sexual intercourse. In the past, virginity was a very highly prized Christian virtue. In the Roman Catholic tradition, it has sometimes been seen as a higher state than being married as virgins were free to devote themselves to God without any distractions.

Vocation a calling from God to lead a particular kind of life. In the history of the **Church**, the word has been used in two ways: **a** for those people called to play certain roles in the Church – as **priests**, **missionaries** or **nuns**, for example. **b** for every **Christian** who has been called by God to serve him in whatever work they do. Today we sometimes speak of a vocation when we mean jobs that are not involved with the Church but which require particular dedication – being a doctor, nurse or teacher, for example.

Votive Mass a **Mass** celebrated by Roman Catholics for a special reason – such as a **Nuptial Mass** following a marriage.

Vows promises that a man or a woman takes freely when they become a member of a religious order. The three vows they undertake are poverty, **chastity** and obedience.

Vulgate the Latin translation of the **Bible** which was widely used in the Western **Church** between the 5th and the 16th centuries. Roman Catholics have used it from the 16th through to the 20th century. It was used, for instance, at the **Second Vatican Council**. ▶See also **Douai Bible**.

Walsingham the most important place of Christian **pilgrimage** in Britain today. The original **shrine** was built in the 11th century as an exact replica of the Holy House of Nazareth, where Jesus lived with Mary and Joseph. It soon became a place of pilgrimage but was destroyed during the **Reformation** in 1538. In the twentieth century Anglican and Roman Catholic shrines have been built and the pilgrims are, once again, flocking to this small town.

Water an extremely important **symbol** in the **Bible**. **1** water is extremely powerful and so it is a symbol of death and destruction. The story of the flood which destroyed the whole world, apart from Noah and his family (Genesis 9), is a good example of this. **2** water is life-giving. In the **New Testament**, the waters of **baptism** wash away **sin** before a person becomes a full member of the Christian community.

Wesley, Charles (1707–88) the greatest hymn-writer in the **Church**'s history and the brother of **John Wesley**. Although he remained faithful to the **Church of England**, his **hymns** were taken up particularly by the **Methodist Church** which was based on the teaching of his brother.

Wesley, John (1703–91) the founder of the **Methodist** movement. Whilst at Oxford, Wesley gathered a group of devout **Christians** together and they became known as the Holy Club or the Methodists. A member of the **Church of England**, John Wesley was converted in 1738 and began preaching in the open air. From 1742 onwards, he travelled the length and breadth of the country on horseback. By the end of his life he is thought to have travelled 250,000 miles in this way.

Whitsun another name for **Pentecost**. Whitsunday follows seven weeks after **Easter Day** and it is when the **Christian Church** celebrates the coming of the **Holy Spirit** to the **disciples** in **Jerusalem** (Acts 2) and the beginning of the Church. The use of white in church for the furnishings and **vestments** acts as a reminder of the white gowns that people used to wear for **baptism**. Whitsun used to be a traditional day for baptising new converts to **Christianity**.

World Council of Churches

this was formed in Amsterdam in 1948 and described itself as 'The fellowship of Churches which accept our Lord Jesus Christ as God and Saviour.' To begin with it was

The symbol representing the fellowship of the Christian Churches.

mainly made up of **Protestant Churches**. Then in 1961 the **Orthodox Church** became a full member. Although it has sent observers since 1961 the **Roman Catholic Church** has never become a full member. This has limited the effectiveness of the organisation.

Worship the acknowledgement by human beings of the supreme worth of God. This is why adoration, praise and thanksgiving all play an important role in Christian worship. Prayer is also used to ask for God's help. In many **Churches**, there are set ways of worship which are written in the service or prayer book. This is called the **liturgy**. In others there is a more flexible approach to services.

APPENDIX

~

The Apostles Creed

I believe in God, the Father almighty, creator of heaven and earth.

I believe in Jesus Christ, his only Son, our Lord.
He was conceived by the power of the Holy Spirit
and born of the Virgin Mary.
He suffered under Pontius Pilate,
was crucified, died and was buried.
He descended to the dead.
On the third day he rose again.
He ascended into heaven,
and is seated at the right hand of the Father.
He will come again to judge the living and the dead.

I believe in the Holy Spirit,
the holy, catholic Church,
the communion of saints, the forgiveness of sins,
the resurrection of the body
and the life everlasting.
Amen.

The Nicene Creed

We believe in one God, the Father, the almighty,
maker of heaven and earth, of all that is seen and unseen.

We believe in one Lord, Jesus Christ, the only Son of God,
eternally begotten of the Father,
God from God, Light from Light,
true God from true God,
begotten, not made,
of one Being with the Father.
Through him all things were made.
For us men and our salvation
he came down from heaven;
by the power of the Holy Spirit

he became incarnate of the Virgin Mary and was made man.
For our sake he was crucified under Pontius Pilate; he suffered
death and was buried.

On the third day he rose again in accordance with the Scriptures;
he ascended into heaven
and is seated on the right hand of the Father.
He will come again in glory
to judge the living and the dead,
and his kingdom will have no end.

We believe in the Holy Spirit,
the Lord, the giver of life,
who proceeds from the Father and the Son.
With the Father and the Son he is worshipped and glorified.
He has spoken through the Prophets.
We believe in one holy catholic and apostolic Church.
We acknowledge one baptism for the forgiveness of sins.
We look for the resurrection of the dead,
and the life of the world to come.
Amen.

Our Father (The Lord's Prayer)

Our Father, who art in heaven,
Hallowed be thy name.
Thy kingdom come.
Thy will be done on earth, as it is in heaven.
Give us this day our daily bread,
And forgive us our trespasses,
As we forgive those who trespass against us,
And lead us not into temptation,
But deliver us from evil.
Amen.
(Matthew 6.9–13)

The Hail Mary

Hail Mary, Full of grace,
the Lord is with thee.
Blessed art thou among women and blessed is the fruit of thy womb, Jesus.
Holy Mary, Mother of God,
Pray for us sinners, now and at the hour of our death.
Amen.

The Beatitudes

Blessed are the poor in spirit;
the kingdom of heaven is theirs.
Blessed are the sorrowful;
they shall find consolation.
Blessed are the gentle;
they shall have the earth for their possession.
Blessed are those who hunger and thirst to see right prevail,
they shall be satisfied.
Blessed are those who show mercy;
mercy shall be shown to them.
Blessed are those whose hearts are pure;
they shall see God.
Blessed are the peacemakers;
they shall be called God's children.
Blessed are those who are persecuted in the name of right;
the kingdom of heaven is theirs.
(Matthew 5.3–10. *Revised English Bible*)